an Amish Family

Illustrated by George Armstrong

an Amish Family

Phyllis Reynolds Naylor

Amereon House
Mattituck

Reprinted 1986 by Special Arrangement

To the Reader

It is our pleasure to keep available uncommon
fiction and to this end, at the time of publication,
we have used the best available sources. To aid
catalogers and collectors, this title is printed in
an edition limited to 300 copies.———— **Enjoy!**

International Standard Book Number 0-8488-0109-1

To order, contact
AMEREON HOUSE, the publishing division of
Amereon Ltd.

Box 1200
Mattituck, New York 11952

Manufactured in the United States of America

To Arlene Stevens Hall

Contents

an Amish Family

Sunrise, Sunset, and In Between

Long before light, a bearded man hitches up his horse and buggy and sets out for an auction twelve miles away. A plump wife in plain black dress and white cap turns on the kerosene lamp and prepares to make breakfast for a dozen people.

As a sliver of sun shows above the edge of the hills, a young woman leaves for her wedding service which will take at least four hours. Small boys in wide-brimmed hats scurry to finish their chores before the bright orange school wagon comes creaking down the road, pulled by a horse and flashing two red lights. Three hundred men wearing coats without buttons gather to build a barn for a friend.

The Amish of Goshen, Indiana, of Iowa City, Iowa, of Lancaster, Pennsylvania, of Wooster, Ohio, and many other communities, begin another day as their ancestors did before them, separate from the world, devout in their faith, and loyal to each other.

In Pennsylvania, in the oldest Amish community in the United States, outsiders refer to the Amish as "the Plain People." The Plain People, in turn, refer to their non-Amish neighbors as "gay" or "fancy" or "English." Tourists gawk at the strange dress and hair styles, at the horses and buggies, at the homes without electricity or plumbing. The Amish, as best they can, mingle only with their own kind, ignoring the stares of outsiders, and believe that the Bible commands them to live apart from those of other faiths. Customs and rules and ceremonies vary from place to place, but the Fishers and Beilers of Pennsylvania, the Millers and Hershbergers of Ohio, and the Yoders and Bontragers of Indiana know exactly what is required of them in order to remain members of their own particular district.

Because of intermarriage among the Amish, the same names go on and on. First cousin marriages are prohibited. Second cousin marriages, though frowned on, are allowed. There are now about 50,000 Amish in the United States, but they share only forty common surnames. Ten common names cover most of the Amish in Pennsylvania.

Twelve-year-old Danny Stoltzfus has more relatives in Lancaster County than he knows of for sure, and a good share of them are Stoltzfuses. Calling them by their first names, as Amish children do, makes it no easier, because given names are often chosen from the Bible, and they too are used over and over again. Benjamin Stoltzfus, Danny's father, is only one of many Benjamin Stoltzfuses, and this is why the Amish use nicknames.

Having unusually curly hair and a curly beard as well, Danny's father has become known as Curly

Ben, not to be confused with Gap Ben Stoltzfus, who lives near a town called Gap, or Short Ben Stoltzfus, who is scarcely as tall as his wife, or Butter Ben Stoltzfus, so named because he puts butter on almost everything he eats—even apple pie.

Besides Danny and his parents, there are five other children, a grandfather, and the mother's unmarried sister living in the house. This is only an average-sized family, possibly even smaller, because most Amish households have seven to nine children, and may include grandparents, a son's wife and children, and an orphaned niece or nephew as well.

As the fog lifts outside the farmhouse, Danny puts on his white shirt and the black trousers which are held up by suspenders. He wears the same sort of clothes to school that he wears about the farm, and the same for Sunday service. When his socks are on and his heavy black shoes, he slips on a sweater that used to belong to an older brother and goes outside to feed the chickens.

As far as Danny can see, the land is still except for the faint black top of a carriage moving slowly down the country road. This is Amish land surrounding the town of Intercourse, which is near the city of Lancaster in Lancaster County. On this November morning, the Pennsylvania fields are brown and gray, for the tobacco is cut and stored, the potatoes dug, the corn stalks shredded, and it is the month for visiting with friends, having company for dinner, and holding weddings.

The chickens are up and waiting. Danny throws feed to the others but stoops to let the small red hen

eat from his hand. He makes a special sound in his throat and she seems to know it is meant for her. She comes quickly over to the narrow-faced boy whose large black hat makes his face look even smaller. Like many of his friends, Danny is especially fond of animals and adopts all kinds of strays for pets. When he was younger, his family would go up in the mountains for picnics. As night fell, they sat quietly "spotting deer," which meant they would stay as still as possible and see how many wild creatures would come near.

The cats are up too—so many that Danny has lost count. One darts out from behind the woodshed, rubbing against his legs, but Danny is interested in something else. He slips into the barn and climbs into the hayloft looking for the pet raccoon he hopes he can train to live there. The animal is not around, but the food which Danny left for him is gone.

As Danny starts to crawl back down, his knee hits something hard under the hay. He digs out a book called *Profiles in Courage,* and instantly Danny knows to whom it belongs and why it is there. He opens the book and reads a scribbled message inside: "To Simon Stoltzfus, from a good friend, Harold Blackman."

From below, in the large white barn, Danny can hear the clank of the milk buckets as his father and two oldest brothers finish milking the fourteen cows. He closes the book quickly and hides it again in the hay. It is not the first time he has found one of Simon's books up here. Danny knows what his fa-

5

ther thinks of outsiders who get friendly with his children and give them books. It is one thing to study hard in school and read the books assigned, but quite another to have books of your own that you don't really need. And knowing how his father would feel, he slides back down the hay, goes into the house for breakfast, and says nothing.

The Stoltzfus house, like most of the other Amish homes, is large, with a sprawling addition built on one side of it called the *Grossdawdy Haus* (granddaddy house) for Danny's grandparents. Amish homes, though often purchased from non-Amish, are rarely sold to those outside the faith. Most farms are passed down from one generation to another, and sometimes three or four generations may live in the house at the same time.

The aging *Grossdawdy* and *Grossmutter* turn the farm over to one of their sons and retire to the *Grossdawdy Haus*, still very much a part of the family. Sometimes the oldest son inherits the farm. But Benjamin Stoltzfus is still a strong man and has many years left to work. His three oldest sons, Noah, Gideon, and Simon, will be ready to start their own farms long before Benjamin stops working, and they will need to have land of their own. It is Danny who will some day take over his father's farm. He knows this as he goes about his daily chores, and does an extra good job because of it.

All of the buildings on the farm are white, down to the woodshed, the milkhouse, the outhouse, and the picket fence. Even the trunks of the trees and the grape arbors have been given a fresh coat of whitewash. The recent painting makes Danny believe that Sarah, his older sister, will be marrying soon. But she won't say for sure till the announcement is made at a Sunday preaching service.

There are dark green shades at all the windows but no curtains. Nor are there pictures or mirrors on the walls of Old Order Amish homes. Some districts allow vividly colored handmade rugs and pillows and quilts. The only decoration in the Stoltzfus home is the brightly colored china and glassware that Rebecca, the mother, keeps in a corner cupboard and on a shelf around the dining room walls. They are not merely for show, but are used whenever there is a crowd for dinner.

The furniture itself is plain. There are no overstuffed chairs and sofas in the living room, nor do the pieces match. Often handmade of varnished natural wood, furniture is passed down from one generation to another, and the rockers in the front room once belonged to Rebecca's grandmother.

Home is the center of Amish life, for this is where everything takes place—births, baptisms, worship services, weddings, and funerals. The kitchen, especially in winter, is the hub of activity. There is no central heat, and the large stove, almost in the center of the huge kitchen, furnishes the heat for the room and adds a little warmth to the bedroom above it. That bedroom belongs to Nancy, the youngest Stoltzfus. The other bedrooms have no heat.

Breakfast is at seven. It is a full meal, and the eight-board table, covered with oil cloth, holds eggs, fried cornmeal mush, liverwurst, cooked cereal, fried potatoes, bread, butter, and apple butter.

Benjamin and his sons are just coming in from rolling the milk cans to the end of the lane where they will be picked up by a commercial milk truck. Danny's father takes his place at the head of the table, Danny to his left, then Simon and Gideon and Noah. Mother and the girls sit on his right with Danny's aunt, Esther Yoder, and Grandfather sits at the far end. All heads bow in silent prayer, and then Benjamin picks up his fork and begins to eat. No meal is started till all are present.

There is no radio or TV to interrupt the quiet of the family breakfast. They talk of the work schedule for the day and glance at the chalkboard on one wall where Rebecca has written reminders of what needs to be done.

Three languages make the Amish trilingual—Pennsylvania Dutch, High German, and English. It is Pennsylvania Dutch which the family speaks at home in their everyday lives—a distinct dialect of the German language and not simply garbled English or German. English spoken in a Dutch manner often sounds strange to a visitor. When it is starting to rain, for instance, the Amishman says, "It is making down." But the tourist industry, which puts out clever Amish sayings, mixes up the words far more than is really done.

The Amish are only a small percent of Americans who speak this dialect. Others include some Lutheran sects, some Mennonites, some Church of the Brethren or Dunkers, and Brethren in Christ. Those groups which speak the dialect but do not dress plain are known as the "gay" Dutch.

English is the second language of the Amish child, but he usually does not learn it until he studies it in school. In informal conversation, language often slips back and forth between Pennsylvania Dutch and English. High German is used only in the preaching services or when the Amish father reads from the old German Bible at bedtime.

"We can start the stripping today, Noah," Benjamin tells his oldest son, referring to the tobacco that is drying in the barn. Stripping the leaves from the plant is a long process, and the whole family will help in the dark winter months while they wait for spring.

"Was thinking of going to the auction up at Sam Lapp's," Noah replies, with a knowing smile.

"That's today, then? Thought it was tomorrow," Benjamin says, but Noah shakes his head.

"Then I'll be going too," announces Danny's mother. "Might be we can pick up a roomful."

Again the smiles go round the table among the older members of the family, and Danny knows for sure now that Sarah is getting married. There could be no other reason for buying a roomful of furniture at an auction than as a wedding present for a daughter.

"Sure would like a set of rockers," Sarah says from her side of the table, and that clinches it. Danny tries to figure out who the groom will be, but that is a big secret in Amish homes.

It is almost eight o'clock, and breakfast ends as it began, with silent prayer. Now it is time for "dressing around" and getting books together for school. Rebecca checks to see that Nancy has on the several layers of clothes needed to keep her warm, and tells Danny to pat his hair down because he looks *stroovlich*. Then the three youngest Stoltzfus children set off on the two mile walk to school.

This Amish family has no electricity or plumbing because it is forbidden in their *Ordnung* (the unwritten rules of their district), but the farm has power nonetheless. Drinking water is lifted from the well in the yard by a water wheel three-hundred yards away. A long wire, fastened to short poles, stretches out across the garden and over the field to the stream, and connecting the pump at the well to the water wheel. By a series of ingenious devices, this rotary motion is converted to a push and pull of the long wire, which makes the pump handle go up and down. Most Amish farms in Lancaster County have three or four hand-dug wells. Windmills are also used in case the streams dry up in a drought.

As Danny crosses the road, his ears pick up the sound of water bubbling in the stream below and the squeak of the wire as it rubs against the posts. Last week his father took him down to the meadow and explained how the counter balance works. The next time it needs adjusting, Danny will try to do it. It makes him feel good to know that he is needed, and each time he is allowed to do work that only his brothers could do before, Danny feels especially proud.

There are about sixty different Amish settlements in North America, and each settlement is divided into church districts. In some, children attend only Amish-run schools, and the school bus is actually a horse-drawn wagon with battery-operated lights. In others, regular school buses take the children to public schools. In some districts, carriage tops must be black. In others, yellow or white or gray is permitted. In some districts, an Amish hymn takes thirty minutes to sing, the dresses of the women are long, and the hat brims of the men are wide. In others, the same hymn takes only eleven minutes to sing, the dresses are shorter, and the hat brims narrower. There are all sorts of rules for the way Danny must live and the way he must dress, and he and his brothers and sisters know exactly what is expected of them.

The school which the Stoltzfus children attend is operated by the Amish themselves. As one-room public schools close down, the Amish buy them from the state. If there are not enough one-room schools to serve all the Amish families who want to attend, an Amish farmer donates a corner of his land and a school is built.

The teacher begins the day by reading verses from Martin Luther's translation of the German Bible, followed by the Lord's Prayer in German. Nancy, a first grader, knows almost no English and must learn to speak it here. Children in the upper grades are taught High German so that they may read the family Bible. The older students help the younger. Sometimes a whole day is devoted to one particular subject.

There is a half hour for lunch, and fifteen-minute recesses in the mornings and afternoons. When the last lesson of the day has ended, some children set off over the fields for home, climbing fences as they go. Others hitch a ride with a non-Amish neighbor in his car.

Nancy is eager to get home and play with the kittens. She takes off at a run, swinging her lunch pail. But Danny and his brother follow the road, and when they reach the end of the Stoltzfus lane and see that the *Sugarcreek Budget* newspaper is still in the mailbox, they know that their parents are not yet home from the auction, so they can put off their chores a little longer.

Simon goes in the house, but Danny heads to the barnyard to check on the calf he has been given to raise. He is satisfied to see it looking strong and plump. He will have to feed the animals before supper and shovel manure into the pile behind the barn, to be used in the spring for fertilizer. Then it will be time for homework and supper around the big table. Benjamin will read from the German Bible and the lamps will go out at nine o'clock, for five in the morning comes early.

There is a creaking noise in the lane, and Danny looks around the corner of the barn to see his parents and Sarah coming up in the family carriage, followed by Noah and Gideon in the hauling wagon, pulled by two work horses. The wagon is loaded down with straight-backed chairs, a table, two rockers, and an iron bedstead, and Danny can see that Sarah is smiling.

2

*M*arriage and *Settling Down*

Sarah is twenty years old and ready to be a wife. From the time she was old enough to stand on a chair in the kitchen and help her mother make pies, Sarah has been learning to cook, to bake, to tend a garden and preserve the vegetables, to keep a house in immaculate order, and to make all her own clothes.

At a Sunday preaching service, which Sarah did not attend, the bishop announced that Cleon Zook and Sarah Stoltzfus planned to marry in two weeks, and before the last hymn was sung, Cleon left the service, unhitched his horse, and rode quickly over to Sarah's house where she awaited the news that they were "published."

Sarah will become Mrs. Cleon Zook, but friends and relatives will continue to call her Sarah. Because there is already another Cleon Zook in the settlement, this new husband will now be referred to as "Sarah's Cleon."

Marriage is the goal of Amish parents for their

offspring, and all social activities and get-togethers for the young are planned with matrimony in mind and plenty of opportunities for getting acquainted. A teenage boy and girl look at each other not merely as friends but as possible mates. While they are free to date whom they choose within their particular Amish order and are doubtless attracted by pretty eyes or a strong physique, they must shrewdly consider the other's health, stamina, and willingness to work. Their mutual goal is to become a debt-free farm family. "Before the empty crib, the horses bite each other," an Amish saying goes, and each knows that for their relationship to succeed, their farm itself must prove a success.

Marriage, more than anything else, keeps the Amish in the faith. Once a man or woman marries and begins a family, surrounded by supporting relatives, traditions, and the work of an unmechanized farm, it is improbable that he or she will leave the church. Whatever their needs or their problems, the young couple have the financial, moral, and physical help of friends and neighbors, and will be reluctant to give it up. For this reason, scarcely any other event is greeted quite so joyously as a wedding.

Danny was told the night before the announcement that his new brother-in-law was to be Cleon Zook. Now that the prospective groom or *Hochzeiter* has moved in with the Stoltzfus family, as is the custom, Danny will have a chance to know him better. There is a tremendous amount of work to be done before the wedding, and Cleon is there to help with the preparations. There are nuts to be cracked, floors to be scrubbed, silverware to be polished, and dishes to be borrowed. But the bridegroom's first assignment is to personally invite all the guests, and these are decided by the parents of the bridal party.

There will be an enormous crowd at the Stoltzfus's home on Sarah's wedding day. Perhaps two hundred or more guests will come for dinner. All the bride's relatives are invited, and neighboring farmers as well, both Amish and non-Amish. If a girl was employed as a maid in a non-Amish home before her marriage, her former employer might also be invited. Often the groom's guests are confined to the members of his immediate family. Children are specifically mentioned if they are included, and some are invited only for the evening's festivities. Honorary invitations are extended to uncles and aunts and neighbors—usually married couples— to serve as cooks and waiters, the one time an Amish man helps in the kitchen.

Sarah will be the first of the Stoltzfus children to marry, even though she is two years younger than Noah. There are times Danny doesn't like the thought of her leaving, but other times when he doesn't care. It's hard for him to imagine Sarah as somebody's wife. Only last summer the kitchen had been full of laughing, teasing girls, as Sarah and her friends got together for a "weeding frolic." The Stoltzfus family, like many other Amish families, sets aside an acre of land on which to raise a particular crop for charity. Teenage girls go from farm to farm watering, weeding, and caring for these acres until harvest time, when they pick the crop, preserve and label it, and distribute it to a nearby "English" (non-Amish) orphanage.

But now Sarah will be married, and much of the giggling and teasing will stop. The day after the wedding, she will put away the long white apron which a girl wears over her dress, and will don a black one instead like those of other married women. Sober work-filled days and evenings will replace the secret midnight rides in Cleon's courting buggy.

Danny had an idea it might be Cleon. Once, when Sarah was going to a Sunday evening "sing," Danny hid in the corn at the end of the lane and saw her get in Cleon's buggy.

Traditionally, at age sixteen, an Amish boy is given a courting buggy (an open buggy without a top), and a beautiful spirited horse. Because there are so few carriage makers left, however, and it takes so long to fill an order for a new buggy, some Amish boys do their courting in the closed family carriage, and Amish fathers sometimes use the courting buggy to do their errands.

The Amish want their young people to pair off and marry, so there is little interference from parents. Nonetheless, courting is done in secrecy and under cover of darkness, because that is the way it has always been. Cleon would have been teased if his friends had found out that he and Sarah were serious about each other, but the parents had known it for some time.

A young man makes the first overtures. He confides to a friend which girl it is that interests him,

and the friend arranges for him to take the girl home from a get-together. If the girl refuses, it is not so bad, because she didn't reject him personally. She merely said no to his friend.

Affection in front of others is avoided. Most friends and many relatives do not know that a couple is thinking about marrying until the bans are posted in the Sunday preaching service. Cleon usually picked Sarah up at the end of the lane, and when he came to the house, it was always late at night after Benjamin and Rebecca were in bed. He simply signaled with a flashlight at Sarah's window, and she went down to see him.

Bundling, or bed courtship, still takes place in some parts of the country, but is generally disapproved of in most districts. Because transportation by horse and buggy is slow and a young man often has to go a considerable distance to visit the girl he likes, it is considered quite proper by some Amish that he stay all night. And rather than sit up in a cold house or waste fuel keeping a room warm for only two people, it is thought only natural that the young couple should simply lie in bed together under a quilt, fully dressed. Because the custom has sometimes led to sexual relations before marriage, however, Amish leaders have tried to stop bundling in many districts. Now most Amish youth do their courting in the sitting room or kitchen, and the boy arrives back at his own home in the early morning.

When the couple decide to marry, the boy tells a deacon of his congregation who goes to the girl's father and asks his consent. This is mostly a formality, since fathers seldom refuse permission. No boy will admit to his friends even then that he is engaged until the announcement is made by the bishop at a preaching.

Amish marriages traditionally take place in November, the month after harvest, when there can be community-wide participation. There may be several weddings in a settlement each week, and most occur on a Tuesday or Thursday (usually Thursday), but no one is quite sure of the reason. Like so many other things, it has always been the custom. Sundays, however, are a day of rest, reserved for preaching services, so Monday allows time to prepare for Tuesday's weddings, Wednesdays are used to prepare for Thursday's weddings, and by Friday and Saturday, it is time to think about Sunday again.

It is now the day before Sarah's wedding, and friends and neighbors are arriving to prepare the chickens and ducks for roasting. Celery will be cleaned, potatoes peeled, potato chips fried in open iron kettles of hot lard, and cakes and pies baked by the dozen. There may be as many as thirty cooks, mostly married couples plus the two closest friends of the groom and two bridesmaids who come as early as seven o'clock. Custom requires that the bridegroom cut off the heads of the fowl. Men pick the pinfeathers, set up trestles on the backless benches to form tables, supply the hot water, and empty the garbage. Women wash and dress the fowl, bake the pies and cakes, and do the dishes.

Cleon seems well liked by both his friends and the older folk, and this pleases Rebecca very much. It is important that a young man get along with his Amish neighbors.

The size of the girl's house and the number of her relatives determine how many guests will be invited. Rebecca realizes that at least two hundred and fifty people, maybe more, will be attending her daughter's wedding and they will have to be fed in shifts. If the bride's house is very small and the guest list is large, the wedding dinner might be held at the groom's house or in the home of a relative, but the bride's family is still responsible for the food and its preparation. The food for a typical Amish wedding may cost $800 or more.

Rebecca knew many months in advance that Sarah and Cleon were serious about each other, and told no one else but her husband and sister. There was, however, an unusually large crop of celery in the garden, traditionally served at Amish weddings, and a few people wondered why Benjamin painted his barn again when it could have gone another year. For several months, Rebecca and her sister had worked to clean up the rooms of the house, and now the big day has arrived and there is thankfully no more time for cleaning.

Sarah is up at five in the morning. It is important that the wedding go smoothly. "A sloppy wedding makes a sloppy bride," the Amish say. The day is clear, and not as cold as it has been. This is good news, because many people will have to wait outdoors and in the barn for their turn at the dinner tables.

There will be no ring, no flowers, no bells, no

bouquet or wedding dress. Sarah is wearing new clothes, and so is Cleon, but the garments are simply Sunday best, and nothing special. The bride's dress is of light blue cotton with a white net organdy kerchief and apron reaching from the high neckline to the full length of her skirt. The outfit is completed with the prayer cap which she wears always over her dark hair.

Before daylight, Cleon and Sarah and their two attending couples go to a neighbor's house where the preaching service and ceremony will be held. Benjamin and Rebecca do not attend, for they are busy supervising the dinner preparations back home.

Three young men called "hostlers" are responsible for seeing that the bridal party reaches the house where the service will be. The hostlers drive the three couples in their buggies which have been polished and painted for the occasion. They are also in charge of the horses and carriages of the guests, which begin arriving at the neighbor's home about seven-thirty. As each carriage pulls up, a hostler gives the driver a numbered slip of paper and writes the same number on the side of the buggy in chalk. Then they park the horses and buggies in the field. Another duty is to pass an empty jug around after dinner and supper are underway. They make a lot of noise collecting change from the guests, which is distributed later among the cooks and waitresses.

As more people arrive, the older folks and children enter by the front door, but single girls go around to the back. Weddings reunite relatives from remote parts of the country, and young people come from distant states to look for mates. The young men are particularly interested in the line of single girls at the back door, and gather to watch them go in.

The guests find Cleon and Sarah already seated. The congregation begins the service by singing hymns from the *Ausbund,* the old Amish hymnbook. Cleon and Sarah go to an upstairs room for a meeting with the church officials while their attending couples wait for them at the stairway. In this conference, the young couple will receive final instructions on the ideals and duties of husband and wife toward each other. When they return, holding hands, one of the attending couples walks ahead of them and the other behind. When they sit, the three young men are facing the three young women, with the attendants sitting on either side of the bride and groom.

As in the usual Sunday morning services, the men sit on one side of the room, the women on the other, facing each other. The men put their hats under their benches, and finally the preaching begins.

Sarah and Cleon have chosen the two preachers themselves from among their favorite preachers in the region, and the sermons praise most of the married people in the Bible. The first preacher usually talks about Adam and Eve to Ruth, and the second preacher will continue to the story of Tobias, which is found in the Apocrypha, fourteen books of the Old Testament which are not included in the Bible. Because the preachers know that the cooks are waiting back at the bride's house, they do not usually

extend the service beyond one o'clock. When the sermons are finished, some guests arise and give personal testimony, telling the bride and groom to be kind to one another.

The marriage ceremony itself, which follows, is quite short. The bishop calls Cleon and Sarah to the front to make their promises to each other, and the groom speaks first.

The bishop then puts the couple's hands together and says, "So we see that Raguel took the hand of the daughter and put it into the hand of Tobias and said: The God of Abraham, the God of Jakob, the God of Isaac be with you and help you together and give you his blessing richly over you, and all this through Jesus Christ. Amen."

Cleon and Sarah are now pronounced husband and wife. The congregation kneels for the closing prayer, the benediction, and a final hymn.

Sarah and her new husband, along with their attending couples, are the first to leave the service. There is no throwing of rice or pranks or laughter. The mood is serious, and Amish weddings are never photographed. When the young people reach the bride's home, the newlyweds go immediately to an upstairs room to wait while their guests assemble below.

The wedding dinner is the most lavish, festive meal which the Amish give, and Danny and his young sister Nancy, surveying the hugh quantities of food from the doorway, have never seen quite so much at one time. A typical wedding dinner might consist of the following:

50 chickens and ducks, each roasted with a quarter pound of butter

veal roasts, with stuffing and gravy

50 pies

several washtubs full of celery and a smaller tub of celery hearts for the bride's table

3 lard cans full of fresh applesauce

7 5-pound fruit cakes, and 18 layer cakes of various flavors, plus two beautiful wedding cakes all done up with nuts and colored candies

25 large bowls of tapioca pudding, 25 of chocolate cornstarch pudding

a case of oranges

50 quart jars of canned fruit

several cases of ginger ale

a washtub full of chowchow

2 washtubs of mashed potatoes

4 lard cans of potato chips

large platters of sausage

fresh bread, candies, jellies, sweet potatoes, fruits, peas, beans, and assorted cheeses

a turkey for the bride's table

The best of everything is reserved for the bride's table, which is placed in the corner most visible to everyone. The bridal corner is called the *Eck*. The bride and bridegroom are highly esteemed, and the occasion is geared for their full enjoyment. When the couple come downstairs for the dinner, Sarah will see the beautiful wedding cakes for the first time, made by her closest friends. There is also a great quantity of candy. The tables are decorated with the fanciest china, but no flowers.

Benjamin Stoltzfus shows the guests to their places while Rebecca supervises in the kitchen. The company sits by age groups. The younger ones and brothers and sisters sit nearest the bride and groom. Church officials are sometimes served in a separate room. Because there is not enough space for all to sit down at once, the men eat first with some of the children, and later the women and the rest of the children will eat. Many of the married women eat in the kitchen.

The bishop gives the signal for silent prayer, and the meal that follows is a joyous occasion, with plenty of talk. All are expected to eat well, and old Eli Bontrager brings along a package of mints to aid his digestion.

The cooks have already eaten, and two couples are assigned to each table to wait on the guests. Opposite the bride and groom sits the *Schnitzler* (carver) who will carve the turkey for them and see that the wedding party is well served. When the first shift of guests have finished, they leave the house and walk around outside to inspect the farm, and the second group comes in to eat. Cleon moves about among the guests, greeting people and offering cigars or candy bars.

Hymn singing continues on through the day. Everyone sings at the wedding dinner except the bride and groom (because of the superstition that to sing today is to weep tomorrow). Some of the hymns are slow, but most are sung to faster beats. Each guest has brought his own small songbook called the *Lieder Sammlungen*. Sarah and Cleon remain at their table while the second group enjoys its dinner, and the merrymaking and visiting goes on.

The older folk head for home about four o'clock, but the younger ones stay on for evening fun. There is much talking and laughter, parlor games, and jokes with the groom. In some locales, beardless boys watch for a chance to snatch the groom away from the bride and chuck him over the fence and into the arms of the waiting married men. Another custom requires the bride to step over a broom—her entrance to matrimony.

Danny thinks he has eaten enough to last a week, but now the tables are being set for supper. Instead of removing the leftover food from dinner, the cooks bring in more platters. Now the young people must come to the table in couples, holding hands in the example of the bridal party, and young boys seem very shy about finding a partner. Simon refuses to ask any of the girls to be his, so he is seized good-naturedly by Gideon and Noah and brought over to Martha Troyer, his second cousin. Embarrassed, he leads her to the table.

The feasting begins again, with meat loaf and ham and noodles. Food will stay on the table as a midnight snack for guests who remain that long. As a special treat, Cleon and Sarah are served baked oysters and also ice cream.

The singing goes on till ten o'clock, and all through the evening Sarah and Cleon send platters of cakes and pies and candies from the *Eck* to their special friends seated in various parts of the house.

The last song sung at Amish weddings is *Guter*

Geselle (Good Friend):

"Good friend, what do you say?
O good friend I tell you—
I tell you what one thing is;
One is God alone,
He who lives and He who soars,
And He who leads the true Faith
In Heaven and on Earth."

Wedding gifts are displayed on the bride's bed, and after supper some of the guests make their own presentations, saying a few funny things about the gift they have chosen. Some of their friends try to embarrass Cleon and Sarah by giving them baby supplies as gifts.

The bride does not object to presents which the strict Amish code does not favor, such as fancy glassware, dishes with colorful designs, or embroidered linen, provided they are useful and non-electrical. It would be considered rude not to accept wedding gifts. Nor does Sarah mind duplicates, for the Amish entertain on such a grand scale that there can never be enough dishes or pans or tablecloths or sheets. Nothing need match, and many of the gifts are handmade rather than costly. If the bride does not receive enough bedding, there will be a quilting party later at her new home to help her make some covers.

Sarah and her husband are particularly lucky, because Cleon's father is presenting them with a farm of their own, a not uncommon wedding gift from a parent. It will be in another Amish district, but still close enough for visiting back and forth. Rebecca is

delighted at the good fortune of her daughter.

Cleon's parents will also give the young couple some basic farm equipment, and Sarah's parents are giving her the furniture which they purchased at auction, as well as a new stove and three cows. Rebecca has already made a quilt for each of her children, to give them on their wedding days, and Sarah's is particularly beautiful. Being the oldest daughter in the family, Sarah will also inherit an antique clock which has been passed down from Rebecca's great grandmother. It has been Sarah's responsibility to wind all the clocks in the house each night, and now she will take the oldest one with her to her new home.

When the evening meal is finally over, the young folk go to the barn to play games and square dance till midnight. When the merrymaking begins to die down, and after most of the guests have gone, Sarah and Cleon retire in private to their part of the house. The two attending couples also spend the night at the bride's home. There are no pranks till the following day. Then, in some districts, it is customary for the bride and groom to do the family washing, and there are all sorts of complications as friends remove parts of the washing machine and do other mischief.

With much laughter, Sarah and Cleon have just hung their second load of wet clothes on the line when Simon and Gideon sneak out from behind the milk house and loosen the rope. The whole wash falls in the dirt and has to be done over.

There is no honeymoon in Amish country, but the next few months are spent visiting the many relatives of each. Often the two families hardly know each other, and this gives Sarah's relatives a chance to meet Cleon, and Cleon's relatives a chance to know Sarah better. Sometimes, during this period, the groom returns to his own home, picking up his bride on weekends and setting off for another round of visiting, staying at the homes of relatives at night. But Cleon stays at the Stoltzfus home until the farm to which they are moving is vacant. They will visit as many as eight or more different relatives each weekend, and will receive another gift at each home as well as much advice.

When spring comes and they are settled, they will

begin rearing their family, for by then new life is often on the way. Despite the large number of wedding gifts, Amish needs are few, and the furnishings of a plain home are sparse. When Cleon and Sarah set out for the house of their own, a single farm wagon will easily transport all that they have.

It has been a good day, an efficiently-run wedding, with much laughter, good feeling, and many friends who have not been seen for a long time. The only unhappy note is that one relative could not be invited, a young cousin named John Byler. He is a particular favorite of Sarah's, and she is sad that he could not be asked. But John is being shunned because he took on worldly ways. Unless he confesses his guilt to the bishop, and the congregation votes him back in, he can never eat at their table again.

This is a tragedy that causes much pain within an Amish family and the community. But obedience to God is even more important than family ties, and because her faith forbids her to associate with the unrighteous, Sarah does not plan to see her cousin and tries hard not to even think about him.

3

t he Amish Way

Benjamin Stoltzfus is going to build a barn. Old
Isaac Esh has had a lot of trouble this year, and when
lightning hit his barn a week ago, it took the livestock too. It is early March, and the worst of the
winter is over. At least three hundred men will come
to the little town of Bird-In-Hand, Pennsylvania,
for the barn raising, and the entire Stoltzfus family
is in the carriages and on the way by six o'clock.

Old Isaac had neither a lightning rod on his barn
nor insurance, for the Amish do not believe in
them. It is God who sends the "gusts," as they call
thunderstorms, and a lightning rod would thwart
God's plans. When Isaac Esh's barn burned to the
ground, the Amish believe, Isaac was bearing the
wrath of God for the whole community. So everyone works to rebuild it, and this is all the insurance
Isaac needs.

The Amish have neither old age pensions nor life
insurance, and they do not accept social security.
There is profound respect for God and for each

other, and when someone is in need, or there is an emergency, the community rallies around him.

Community effort, the power of the organized crowd, is the chief characteristic of this cultural group, which is probably stronger than any other communal society in America. Unity is the foundation of Amish life. Unlike modern communes which have existed for only a few years, where members come and go and the purpose and rules are changed as individuals see fit, the Amish order, founded in the Anabaptist faith, dates back to the 1600's. Those who leave the order are the exceptions, and the rules are followed unquestioningly, changing slowly, if at all.

A settlement is composed of all the Amish families living in one large area. The settlement is divided into church districts. There are usually four ordained men in each district—a bishop, two preachers, and a deacon. The size of each district is determined by the maximum number of families that can be accommodated at the Sunday preaching service.

The bishop baptizes, marries, buries, and expels members or receives them back according to the vote of the baptized members. He also takes his turn preaching the main sermon on Sundays. Bishops do not have conferences or any kind of central organization. Each is supreme in his own district of 50 to 100 families.

The two preachers preach to the people about the ways of God without any special training, though they do make use of a published handbook for preachers. The deacon, or minister to the poor, is responsible for widows and orphans, and he collects alms. He looks after the welfare of those who have misfortunes, settles quarrels, and reads scriptures at the service. He also assists in church ceremonies, but does not preach.

Bishops, preachers, and deacons are ordained for life until they are old or weak, or unless they misbehave. Bishops generally may not move from one district to another if there is dissatisfaction. Preachers and deacons are freer to do so if they have the approval of their district.

The four men are chosen by biblical lot. When there is a vacancy, a number of candidates are suggested by officers of the church and members of the congregation. At a service they are all called to the front of the room where there is a table with as many Bibles as candidates. When all have taken a Bible, they are told to turn to a given text. The one who finds a slip of paper at that page is now the new officer of the church. The Amish believe that the Lord will select the best man in this way. The congregation abides by the choice, even if the chosen officer turns out to be unpopular, for there is no way to rid themselves of a poor leader unless he becomes very ill or commits a serious offense. Church officials who are too lenient with the young, however, face the criticism of older members.

All baptized males are eligible for election to one of these offices, and each male, when baptized, must promise to accept office if the lot should befall him. Each woman promises to bear with whomever shall be called to be leader. Preachers are always chosen from within the district and never from another congregation. The district itself possesses no property other than benches and hymnals, has no funds, and collects no tithes. Individual members voluntarily contribute money or labor to the needy in time of emergency.

A barn raising is not the only kind of mutual aid which the Amish offer. Many times during the year, Benjamin will take off his work coat, roll up the sleeves of his homemade shirt, and help a neighbor saw wood, erect a milk house, paint his kitchen, build a fence, or butcher his steers. His wife, Rebecca, will be called on to make quilts, clean another's house, or help out with baking, cooking, or preserving fruits and vegetables. When disaster strikes an Amish household, the neighbors do that family's chores for them, take care of their children, and harvest their crops. When a barn burns down, each household is assessed as needed.

It is full light by the time Benjamin's buggy pulls in the lane at the Esh farm, with Gideon and some of the others in the carriage behind. Danny, sitting on the front seat between his parents, has not seen so many buggies since Sarah's wedding. Though only some of the men are carpenters by trade, all have participated in barn raisings before and will work under the direction of a master carpenter. Most of the men are farmers, but others work in factories, lumber mills and butcher shops. Some are day laborers, railroad workers, and a very few are blacksmiths.

Old Isaac is in the field welcoming his friends and helping direct traffic as more horses and buggies pull in. Some of the same neighbors were here to help fight the fire and carry away debris. Now they are back to build a new barn. Forty women came over the day before to start the cooking, and now an old bus rumbles in from a distant town, packed with Amish men in their working clothes.

By seven o'clock everyone is there—women arriving with homemade cakes and pies, men with their own tools. In the house, the women prepare the chickens, fry potato chips, and make lemonade. In the field, the men put the framework together, not with nails but with pegs because the barn will last longer. In the lane and around the house, children chase each other and take turns pulling a toy wagon. Even old Jonas, Danny's grandfather, has come along to sit and watch the work and talk with the other men his age. A barn raising is a holiday of sorts and one of the few get-togethers in which there are no religious overtones to inhibit laughter and horseplay.

There is much joking going on as the men work. The foundation has already been laid, so they divide into groups and begin erecting the main timbers and framework. Their muscles strain as they raise the beams, for it takes sixteen men to get one in place.

The first break comes about ten, and girls scurry around with sandwiches and lemonade and doughnuts as a midmorning snack. At home, they call it the "ten o'clock piece," and the wife or daughter brings a snack out to the field in a basket. By noon, the men are hungry again. The sun has been hot, despite the March breeze, and the temperature is climbing. The women decide to serve lunch outdoors on long tables made of planks placed on sawbucks and spread with tablecloths.

The men and older boys eat huge quantities of everything, and there is much variety. The usual Amish diet is rich in fats and carbohydrates, and contains much gravy, potatoes, fried foods, and pastries. Today the work crew feasts on bread and butter, grape jelly, apple butter, mashed potatoes and gravy, fried ham, macaroni, baked beans, coffee, cole slaw, pickles, pickled melon, chicken stewed with celery, sliced tomatoes, cheese, scalloped corn, cracker pudding, peaches, fried hamburger, English walnut pie, angel food cake, and the heavy, molasses-sweet shoofly pie.

But it isn't long before the men are back to work again, and Danny helps his father and older brothers by carrying tools back and forth as they need them, watching to see how it's done, and trying some of the work himself under his father's direction. As the siding is hammered in place, Benjamin smiles to himself. When Levi Beiler tries to pick up his claw hammer, he finds it nailed to the floor of the barn, and Danny's father breaks into a loud laugh as Levi struggles with it, to the amusement of the other men, who have pranks of their own in mind. It is laughter that makes the work lighter, and responsibility for each other that gives it meaning.

As head of his family, Benjamin's goal is to live a simple, work-filled life in obedience to God, to work

to overcome obstacles, and to show courage in face of adversity. A barn raising fulfills all three. To live, grow, and pass on the Amish traditions to his children is all that Benjamin hopes to accomplish. As an Amishman, he believes that he was born to till the soil. He regards himself not so much a landowner as a guardian of the land for future generations, for God and nature are inseparable. When he cuts down a tree for firewood, he plants another so that some day Danny will have the use of it. The operation of the farm is his responsibility, and his wife is in charge of the house. The Bible, he believes, exhorts him to replenish the earth and bring forth a good harvest, and that is what he does, without question.

The Amish are not taught to debate or reason or question. "The peasant believes only his father," is an Amish saying which sums up this attitude. Benjamin is the stern patriarch of his household, and his discipline is likely to be severe when he is disobeyed. Knowledge of the Bible and practical farming skills are all that he holds important. He puts his faith in God, follows the rules of his order, and hopes for the best. To obey the *Ordnung*, the unwritten rules of his order, is to have a living hope of salvation, he believes. To disobey is to die.

Self-denial is part of the code, for the Amish believe that restrictions and hardships in this earthly life are necessary. The harder they toil, the more assured they are of eternal salvation. Thus there is no place for electricity or modern plumbing or power machinery or overstuffed furniture to make their lives easier. They look not for rest, but for noninterference from outsiders so that they may live their lives as God wills it. They also believe in the possibility of real suffering for their religious beliefs, as their ancestors suffered before them, and teach their young to be courageous for whatever may lie ahead.

Religion, to the Amish, is complete obedience to the commands of the Scriptures in every part of their lives. Christ is regarded as a *Wegweiser* (one who shows the way), and is not just to be worshipper for His own sake. The Bible is final, authoritative, and decisive in all disputes. The Amish do not read and study it as a whole, however, but select those passages which are most suited to their needs.

Some of the most used passages are these:

Rom. 12:2 "And be not conformed to this world: but be ye transformed by the renewing of your mind, that ye may prove what is that good, and acceptable, and perfect, will of God."

II Cor. 6:14 "Be ye not unequally yoked together with unbelievers: for what fellowship hath righteousness with unrighteousness? and what communion hath light with darkness?"

Matt. 18:17 "And if he shall neglect to hear them, tell it unto the church, but if he neglect to hear the church, let him be unto thee as an heathen man and as a publican."

I Cor. 5:11 "But now I have written unto you not to keep company, if any man that is called a brother be a fornicator, or covetous, or an idolater, or a drunkard, or an extortioner; with such an one no not to eat."

Exod. 20:4 "Thou shalt not make unto thee any graven image, or any likeness of any thing that is in heaven above, or that is in the earth beneath, or that is in the water under the earth."

From these and other verses, the Amish developed their faith and their way of life. Though the details of their observances vary from community to community, the following are universal among most Old Order Amish: separation from the world, hard work, refusal to go to war, self-denial, uniformity of dress and transportation, attitude against law, refusal to buy life insurance or to accept social security, limited schooling, submission to bishops and deacons, fellowship and feasting, and excommunication and shunning.

Religion and custom have become one, and custom is sacred. Tradition guards against confusion and disorder which result when new ideas invade the community. The rules are honored and followed. Only rarely are they examined or challenged. Customs are good because they are old, the Amish believe, and therefore they are authentic or true. How or why the rules came to be in the first place is not important to them. The Amish firmly believe that modern civilization will come to terrible ruin, and that only they have a chance at salvation.

The March afternoon has become unseasonably warm. Around the barn, draped over sawhorses or thrown in the grass are the black work coats of the men. Vests and sweaters too are shed, for the younger men wear layers of padding under their suit jackets to keep warm. Only the old men wear greatcoats or overcoats when it is cold.

Amish clothing is a simple form of apparel in the same style as that worn by the common people of the sixteenth and seventeenth centuries. Besides his work coat, or sack coat, Benjamin owns a black frock coat for Sunday best, called a *Mutze*. Many of his clothes are made by Rebecca, but some he buys in the Lancaster stores which sell them.

The sack coat which Benjamin has thrown on the grass has no lapels or pockets. Nor do any of his garments have zippers. His broadfall trousers have no fly, but button along the top and down the sides—"barn-door britches," as some call them. They are held up by leather suspenders. Work pants are sometimes made to end high up on the calf, since many Amish men go barefoot in their fields and have no need for pant legs dragging in the dirt. Shoes have high tops.

Amish men like their suits fitted loosely. An ordinary coat can be worn on Sundays or for work, but the *Mutze* is always worn to the preaching service following adult baptism. The *Mutze* is longer than the ordinary coat and has a split tail. Outer garments fasten with hooks and eyes. Being pacifists, the Amish are opposed to buttons on coats because Prussian military officers once wore fancy buttons, though in some communities buttons are allowed on work coats. Shirts, however, can have buttons, and sometimes colors are allowed, but no prints or designs. Neckties are taboo, but in some districts a bow tie is permitted on occasion, as are white elastic armbands and pocket watches.

Straw hats can be worn in summer, but black felt hats are the rule in winter, with no less than a three-inch brim. Strict Amish can be distinguished from the more liberal orders by the width of the brim of the hat and the band around the crown. Older men like flat-topped hats with plain brims, but some of the younger ones wear round tops, "pork pie" style, with rolled brims. Younger men also prefer blue denim store-bought jeans, standard—not western—style. Leather belts are forbidden. Rubber boots and overshoes are permitted, but not rubber suspenders. Amish men must not comb their hair, but simply pat it in place, and the district decides what length it should be. It must be parted in the middle, if at all.

Custom must sometimes give way to practicality. Manufacturers are slowly discontinuing items on which the Amish depend, because the market is so small. Flat straw hats and long capes are now difficult to find, and in some districts corduroy jackets are becoming the standard item for cold weather among the men.

Amish men appear without their hats only in a house or a school, or at the Sunday meeting. Once a man becomes a member of the church and is baptized, he lets his beard grow and shaves only his upper and lower lip. Beards are required for all married men, but mustaches are taboo. In some dis-

tricts, the men are permitted to smoke cigars or pipes, but cigarettes are largely forbidden.

Benjamin Stoltzfus does not question the decisions of his bishop or the rules of the *Ordnung*. The Amish, educated only to the eighth grade, interpret literally whatever Biblical verses they accept, and the chief message of all the verses is the warning to separate from worldly things. Separation demands social, political, and religious avoidance of non-Amish people, but business with outsiders is permitted provided an Amishman doesn't become partners with them.

Benjamin is also allowed to ride in a neighbor's car when going to town if he likes. He may ride the bus when traveling long distances, or he may hire a non-Amishman to drive him, offering to pay whatever bus fare would have been. As long as he himself owns no automobile, he is permitted to ride in the cars of others. The Amish see a difference between using something and owning it.

Amish sects vary in their rules, but the most common taboos across the United States are electricity, telephones, central heating systems, automobiles, or tractors with pneumatic tires. Hooks and eyes rather than buttons must close coats, and horses must be used for farming and travel. There is to be no formal education beyond the eighth grade.

On matters which involve their families or their way of life, such as a county or school bond issue, the Amish register and vote in large numbers. Although some are quite aware of world events, most lack interest in anything beyond their own family, farms, congregations, and principles, and therefore do not vote at all. They swear no oaths and do not, as a group, support church projects, colleges, publishing houses, hospitals, or relief organizations except their local congregations. The Amish are sensitive to the sufferings of other people, however, and are generous contributors to foreign relief, as well as charitable to other non-Amish closer to home.

Amishmen take up no arms in defense of themselves, nor do they pursue their attackers. Many do not lock their doors. Thieves have robbed Amish homes and gangs have thrown stones and bricks through their windows. Some have even set fire to Amish barns.

A year ago, many head of cattle were stolen from a farm near the Stoltzfuses, and then sold. The farmer refused to accept the money which the sheriff recovered or to prosecute the thieves. The Bible verse telling believers to "turn the other cheek" is not merely something to recite on Sundays, but becomes a way of life.

Benjamin has as little to do with the government as possible. He does not keep track of news from Washington, of foreign wars, or of international problems, and the Stoltzfus family ignores national holidays. They do not object to paying taxes, but they accept no welfare of any kind. They restrict crop acreage voluntarily when requested, but refuse to accept government compensation for not planting. They do not want to grow rich. When oil was discovered once on some Amish farms in Kansas, the owners sold the farms and moved to another place.

Benjamin Stoltzfus knows where he stands in

relation to his family, his neighbors, the bishop, and the Amish faith. Like the majority of Amish fathers, he is a shrewd businessman, but he also has sincerity and integrity. A handshake is all that is necessary to seal an important agreement with his neighbors. Those who cause trouble are disciplined within the community. Laziness is not tolerated, and an Amishman could not go for long living off the work of others.

If a hardship is severe, however, the district comes forward with aid. No Amishman ever appeared on the relief rolls during the Depression. There are no very rich nor very poor people among the Amish, but rather a strong sense of togetherness and a willingness to help each other.

It is now four o'clock, and the huge barn is almost finished except for interior work which will be done later by professional Amish carpenters. It is a two-story 40x64 foot structure, with twelve yokes for cows, six stalls, and two haymows. Two men have been injured, but neither seriously, and Isaac Esh is grateful for that. One sprained his back while lifting a beam and another hurt his foot when a hammer fell on it from above. Men have been killed at barn raisings, falling off the high crossbeams, but most accidents consist of nothing worse than a bruised thumb or splinters.

Had Isaac had to pay to have his barn built, it would have cost him thousands of dollars for the labor. He gets it done for nothing. But he will repay it by helping his neighbors when they need it as they have helped him.

There are perhaps two or three barn raisings a year. Amishmen make good builders and also good wrecking crews, for they save every usable item.

It is time to go home now, and the women are rounding up the children. Benjamin stops at the pump to wash, pouring a dipper of water over his entire head to cool himself. When he has dried his face and hands, he reaches for his hat, but finds it gone. With a shout, one of the men points to the top of the barn. There is Benjamin's hat on the highest rafter, and Levi Beiler is chortling as he drives off in his buggy. Rebecca and the children laugh too as Benjamin goes into the barn to retrieve it, but Danny races ahead, shinnies up to the rafters, and throws the hat down.

At home, the cows are milked for the evening and then Benjamin does no more. It is time for rest. He sits down in a straight-backed rocker with the weekly newspaper, *The Budget,* and relaxes. Published in Sugarcreek, Ohio, this newspaper carries news from Amish people all over the country—who was born, who died, who married, and who is visiting. There is news of crops, of droughts, of floods, and of anything else that interests the farmer and his family. For many Amish, it is the only way they keep in touch with friends and relatives in distant states and communities.

Once an Amishman joins the church and gives up frivolous living, there is not much left which he can do strictly for fun, nor is there much time for it even if there were. Besides barn raisings, company dinners, and weddings, auctions are greatly looked forward to, for all work stops and everyone goes whether it is a household sale or a cattle sale. There is usually a ball game going on in an adjoining field, and if the auction is a really big one, children are excused from school.

Other than these pleasures, however, and those of family and feasting, the Amish father gets his enjoyment out of uniting with the community. In the uniformity of its customs, the likeness of appearance, the sameness of setting and activity, the closeness of other Amish farmsteads, and the uniform goals, purposes, thoughts and beliefs, Benjamin finds strength, and in this strength is his satisfaction.

4

growing Up, and the Other Sort of People

From the time she was quite small, Nancy Stoltzfus learned that her family was very different from those outside the Amish settlement. Persons were divided between *unser Satt Leit* (our sort of people) and *anner Satt Leit* (the other sort of people), and she never had any doubt that the Amish way was best.

Inside the familiar house, around the big farm, and in the company of her many dozen relatives, Nancy feels loved and protected. Outside the community, however, surrounded by "English" people and tourists, she is somewhat uncomfortable and shy, and will feel even more self-conscious and resentful of their stares as she grows older.

Their language, for one thing, is different from hers. None of her own family speaks English at home unless a non-Amish visitor comes by. Rebecca is glad that her daughter is learning English at school, but that is all she wants her to know of outside ways.

Today, Nancy needs new shoes, which will be

exactly like the old ones—plain black with laces. When the weather becomes too warm for comfort, she will simply go barefoot except for Sunday service. While they are in Lancaster shopping, Rebecca will purchase some black stockings for herself, as well as many yards of blue and green and violet cotton from which she will make more dresses. Perhaps she will also buy a little soft wool for baby clothes, because Sarah is expecting her first child in October.

Amish children wear miniatures of their parents' clothing, though Nancy's apron is white while her mother's is black. On Sundays, Nancy wears a starched black prayer bonnet tied under her chin with a floppy bow. In cool weather, she wears a long black shawl which falls the entire length of her dress. Occasionally a mother will choose cloth with a very tiny figure on it for a small daughter, but now that Nancy is in first grade, she looks like all the other girls in the one-room school. Each wears dresses of rainbow colors, except for the brighter hues such as orange or red or yellow. Many of the clothes she wears are hand-me-downs from cousins, and a few were once Sarah's, which Rebecca has saved.

Rebecca makes all her children's clothes until the girls are old enough to make their own and the boys reach sixteen. Danny is looking forward to his first store-bought suit, but it will be several years yet. Even then, it will be made by a seamstress neighbor who sells her plain-style clothes to the stores in town.

Much as Nancy dislikes the tourists, (she was

even found making faces at them last year when someone tried to take her picture) , going to town is a welcome change, especially when they go to Lancaster. She scrambles in the back of the buggy, rolls up the canvas so she can see out, and settles down for the ride while her mother sits up front and drives the horse.

It is a pleasant ride through the rolling farm country, and like other Amish children, Nancy amuses herself by singing and watching the clouds of dust roll out behind the big metal wheels of the buggy. Her mother sings as she works in the house, and men often sing in the fields. It is a pleasure they enjoy, and the Amish are particularly adept at making play of their work. Because there is such a tremendous number of jobs to do and so little time for anything else, work becomes an excuse for a get-together. Men joke and play pranks while they build a barn, women laugh and chat while they sew a quilt or can their vegetables. Husking bees have been a tradition, as well as weeding frolics.

The Stoltzfus buggy passes the road leading to the village of Intercourse and heads on toward Lancaster. Nancy clutches her dime and thinks about what she will buy. She receives no allowance for the work she does about the house, but is usually given money for candy when they go to town. At home she has a small bank for the pennies she receives now and then.

"*Denki*" (thank you) , Nancy says when she receives a gift, or "*Willkomm*" (you are welcome) , when someone thanks her, but these are the few words of etiquette which she knows. Polite expressions are seldom used in an Amish home, but neither are angry words. Because each person assumes only the best of intentions from others, such expressions as "Excuse me," or "I'm sorry," are considered unnecessary. Sometimes, when someone bumps another, he will say "Oops!" to show that it was accidental, but usually the Amish feel no need to apologize for the jostles of everyday living unless in the company of outsiders. When Grandfather belches at the table, which Amish frequently do, it is considered a sign of good appetite, and who should apologize for that? Children address all their grown relatives by their first names except for their parents and grandparents, and respect for one's elders is shown simply by obedience.

This is not to say, however, that Nancy never misbehaves or that she is never punished. Benjamin's discipline is strict, and there are a number of things he simply does not tolerate from his children. Profanity is one. Temper tantrums, making faces, name calling, and sauciness are rare because they are followed by punishment. Likewise, pouting or responding reluctantly to a request are followed by smacking with the palm of the parent's hand, a switch, a razor strop, or sometimes a buggy whip.

The emphasis, however, is on responsibility rather than obedience. Parents stress the satisfaction one gets in doing a job well and contributing to the family welfare. It is a big day when a child is allowed to do work that his older siblings can do. At six, Nancy has already learned to bake cookies and embroider simple designs on pillow cases.

Out of sight of their parents, Amish children have occasional quarrels among themselves, sometimes leading to fist fights. Inside the house, however, such squabbles are expressed mildly, either by not answering when spoken to or by speaking to a brother or sister as little as possible.

In Lancaster at last, Rebecca hitches the horse. Taking Nancy's hand in her own, she starts down the sidewalk to the clothing store, and pretends not to notice the curious stares of tourists who have come to Lancaster County for spring vacation. Two "English" women, standing on one corner, offer Nancy a piece of candy as she passes, but the small girl frowns, her mouth set, and Rebecca leads her quickly on by.

Tourists are no favor to the Amish. Besides intruding on their way of life and posing a traffic hazard to the Amish in their buggies, the attractions of Lancaster and the Pennsylvania Dutch have caused land prices to soar. Land around Intercourse is 90% Amish-owned. With a population that is now topping 10,000 in the county, the Amish need even more land for farming, but find prices too high. Land that sells for $300 an acre in other counties can bring $3,000 in Lancaster County. The high prices are due to the demand for farmland, and are helped along by a tourist industry that keeps buying farm plots for tourist attractions and accomodations.

Every year, from early June till late October, thousands of tourists converge on Lancaster County, which now ranks among the top twenty tourist attractions in the country, according to the American Automobile Association. One Amishman, who lives along Route 340 between Bird-in-Hand and Intercourse, says it can take fifteen minutes to get his buggy out of his farm lane.

Perhaps what is resented most is the insensitivity of some of "the other sort of people." Like many travelers, they are often intent on finding what they came to see and of taking back a souvenir of their trip, regardless of the feelings of the Amish.

Those who confine themselves to the shops and other attractions which are open for their benefit, who drive cautiously along the road and admire the big white barns and the green-shaded houses from a distance, and who do not try to photograph their children are the most easily tolerated. But there are others, and it is sometimes all Rebecca and Benjamin can do to keep their tempers. The Old Order Amish believe very firmly in the Biblical commandment, "Thou shalt make no graven image," and photographs, to them, are exactly that. It is against their religion to make an image, especially of themselves, to keep and admire, or for anyone else to admire. And they do not appreciate tourists who refuse to respect their beliefs.

Rebecca remembers well Nancy's first week of school. Having been taught to cover her face and turn away when a tourist attempted to photograph her, Nancy noticed the car which was coming slowly down the road behind her as she started home, and she was a little sorry she had run on ahead of Simon and Danny.

The driver rolled down his window and held out a quarter.

"Here, dear," he said, as a woman got out the other side, hurriedly focusing her camera. "Just stand still and look this way for a moment, will you?"

With a wary glance at the tourists, Nancy turned back to the road and went on faster than before. The car moved along beside her.

"Just a minute, honey," the woman called out. "You want some cookies? I've got some in the car."

But Nancy went on.

"Get back in," the man said to the woman, and after the door slammed, the car went on and disappeared.

Nancy had thought they were gone, but when she reached the crest of the hill, she saw the car parked below. This time the man and woman were standing in the middle of the road, blocking her way.

Lifting her lunch bucket to shield her face, heart pounding, Nancy leaped the ditch and started out across the field, apron flapping, black-stockinged legs flying.

"Hey! We weren't going to hurt you!" shouted the man, but Nancy did not stop until she reached the barn and sat down gasping for breath beside her father. And Benjamin glowered at the car which was now moving slowly away out on the road.

Since then, Nancy has become better at evading tourists, and sometimes makes a game of it, almost enjoying her mad dash over the field to the security of the farmyard, outwitting "the other sort of

people" who seem to have no manners at all.

Many houses and Amish shops post signs saying "No photographs" or "No tourists," but travelers don't always obey and seem to take special delight in securing a forbidden photo. Turning the other cheek, however, is as much a commandment as not making graven images, and the Amishman is glad when he can suppress his anger and handle the situation.

And so it is that when the father reads the old German Bible before bedtime, and the mother sews or works at braiding rugs, and the children play at checkers or study, Nancy feels again the closeness of the family group and considers herself fortunate to be a part of it. The tourists are not envied, and she gets comfort from the steady purring of the gas lantern and the rhythmic tick of the mantel clock.

The young do not spend all their time working, for parents realize that they must be allowed to romp and play and get together with others their own age. Though Amish youngsters get satisfaction from the work they do, and have learned to turn a big job into play, there are special things to do depending on the season. In the winter there is ice skating, marshmallow toasting and singing around a bonfire, as well as sledding, ice hockey, sleigh rides, and fox and geese. In the summer the children enjoy wading, fishing with a hook and a piece of string, tug of war, hiking, high jumping, and chasing butterflies. The Amish do not have many toys, and most of what they own is homemade. Cards are taboo, but checkers and chess are permitted. Kickthe-can and baseball are favorite games, and Nancy's friends enjoy hide-the-thimble, hopscotch, jumping rope, and picking flowers. It is also permissible to go to the zoo and watch the animals. Older children enjoy *botching,* in which two persons seated on chairs clap hands and knees alternately in various ways as rapidly as they can while their feet keep time to a tune.

There is a lot of laughing and teasing and joking among Amish children. In adolescent years, all play takes place in segregated groups of either boys or girls, each trying to outsmart the other with some practical joke. And there are holidays to which they all look forward.

Most Amish holidays are religious. They are not observed by formal assembly, however, but by refraining from normal work and staying home. Twice a year the Amish fast—in spring and in fall—but the fast is limited to breakfast only, a real sacrifice for a hard-working Amishman. They eat a noon dinner and supper as usual. The fast days prepare them for communion, which takes place on the Sunday following the fast.

Easter is another holiday which the Amish observe, and so is Easter Monday. Whitsunday is the 11th Sunday after Easter, the day of Pentecost, and is also called Whitsuntide. The Amish celebrate Whitmonday as well. Forty days after Easter is Ascension Day, another holiday, and on this day the Amish traditionally come to town in large numbers.

Thanksgiving and New Year's Day are holidays. And of course there is Christmas which lasts two days. There are so many friends and relatives to see that they couldn't all be visited in one day, and December 26th is just another Christmas. Usually families take turns inviting either the mother or the father's relatives of which there may be a hundred on one side alone.

On the day before Christmas, school closes early in the afternoon. Though Christmas is kept simple and unadorned, it is still a time of excitement. There are no wreaths and no tree, but the children know that spicy cookies are being made in secret while they are in school, and that parents and older brothers and sisters are hurrying to finish the homemade gifts which will be exchanged.

In the clean white house, tiny branches are cut from pine trees and twisted into circular nestlike shapes, with a tiny candle placed in the center. These decorate the table, mantel, and window sills. The rooms are filled with the aroma of good food, for the Christmas menu includes duck and turkey, potatoes and gravy, pepper kraut, corn and beans, mince pie, chocolate pudding, and nut cakes.

Before going to bed on Christmas Eve, the younger Stoltzfus children set dishes at their places on the table, and later Benjamin and Rebecca fill the dishes with nuts and candy.

On Christmas morning, lots are drawn to see who opens a present first. When all have had a turn, the family draws lots again to see who opens a present first the next time around, and this continues until all the gifts are opened.

Amish children have nothing like the huge toy

63

collections which "English" children often get, but the toys they do receive are treasured, and they care for them well. Last Christmas Danny received a wagon made by his father, a catcher's mitt, hard candy, a sweater, pocketknife, gloves, and a scarf. Nancy got her heart's delight—a rag doll made by Rebecca with a complete Amish wardrobe, and a roller-scooter made by Noah. Next Christmas there will be still another new member in the family besides Cleon, and even more presents to make.

"Let's stop at the baby things, just to see how small," Rebecca tells Nancy as they enter the clothing store. Sarah's coming baby will be Rebecca's first grandchild, and it has been a long time since she made clothes that tiny.

Compared to the small booties on the baby counter, Nancy's feet look almost big. As they settle themselves on the seats in the shoe department, Rebecca unties her daughter's laces and thinks how much she has grown. Soon there will be no small child left in the house.

An "English" woman with a girl about Nancy's age sits down in the same row. In their stocking feet, the two small girls eye each other, wiggling their toes and giggling shyly. Rebecca exchanges a smile with the girl's mother.

"They grow up so fast," the woman says. "I bought her these shoes four months ago and she's outgrown them already."

"I know," Rebecca says sympathetically. "And each time they are more expensive."

The clerk returns with two boxes tucked under

his arm. On Nancy's feet he places the plain black shoes with the stiff high tops. On the English girl's feet he puts a pair of red patent leather shoes with gold buckles.

Awkwardly the two girls clump around for a minute in their new shoes, each staring curiously at the other's. As their mothers pay for the purchases at the cash register, Nancy and her new friend stand side by side at the big mirror to see who is the taller.

From time to time, as Rebecca finishes her shopping, Nancy catches sight of the little girl in the red shoes and waves.

"I like her," Nancy says in Pennsylvania Dutch as they start the slow ride home again.

"She was very nice," Rebecca agrees, and wishes that her daughter's experiences with outsiders were always so pleasant.

5

f *rom Past to Present*

There is a funeral in New Holland. Friends and relatives from the surrounding towns of Goodville, Intercourse, Ephrata, Blue Ball, and Paradise make their way to the home of Jonas Stoltzfus's sister, a woman in her eighties who died of a heart ailment.

Danny sits quietly beside his grandfather as the horse turns up the lane. Old Jonas is silent, and his gnarled hands hold the reins loosely, for the horse knows from years of visiting that this road is familiar. Danny wonders what his grandfather is thinking. He knows that some day there will be a similar funeral for Jonas himself, that the long line of carriages will be turning in the Stoltzfus lane, and it will be grandfather who lies in the simple pine box in his dress coat and white broadcloth shirt.

Jonas's sister, Martha, lived with her daughter's family. She had been seriously ill for several weeks, and there were many callers during that time. They entered the door without knocking, shook hands with the others present, and sat down quietly. When

Martha's daughter came out of the sick room, she talked with a few of the visitors and the others listened. There were long periods of silence.

An Amish death is a sober occasion, but the grieving family is soon surrounded by helpful friends. The news travels rapidly, usually conveyed by the milk truck driver, but sometimes the word is spread by a rider who goes from house to house.

Almost at once people began arriving at the home of Martha's daughter, for neighbors and friends relieve the family of all work and responsibilities. Young men took over the farm chores, and a married couple took over the house, making arrangements for food. The closest kin were free to spend their time in meditation and quiet conversation in the living room around the bier where the body lay.

Funerals are held on the third day following death. Most Amish groups have the body embalmed by a non-Amish undertaker. The coffins are made by Amish carpenters, plain boxes with no side handles, wider in the middle than at the squared-off ends. Many have no lining at all, but Martha's is lined with white cotton. She is dressed in a faded blue dress, with white organdy cape. It is the same dress she wore on her wedding day, slit unobtrusively down the back so that it will fit.

There have been friends and relatives in the house constantly since the old woman died, to help and console. Some came to sit up all night around the coffin while the family members went to bed. Young people gathered at the home the evening before to sing.

Now, as Danny enters the house beside his grandfather, he finds the downstairs already opened into one large room, and benches set up for the service. Amish homes are built with removable partitions between downstairs rooms so that many people can fit inside. When a very large crowd is expected, funerals are sometimes held in a barn. The congregation sits inside, and the body is laid on the wide earthen approach to the big double doors. But here in this house, the unpainted coffin rests on a pair of wooden sawhorses. There are no flowers.

The service starts at ten o'clock, and lasts for almost two and a half hours. There are several speakers who admonish the young not to put off joining the church, lest they die before they are baptized and lose all hope of salvation. The sermons are not eulogies to Martha, but are personal messages directed to the congregation. There is no singing. When the service is over, those present are invited back to the house for dinner after the burial.

Walking between his mother and his grandfather, Danny goes up with the others to view the body once more. There is sorrow and tears, but little audible weeping. Four to six pallbearers have been selected by the family. Their duty is to dig the grave, assist with the seating arrangement at the funeral, open and close the coffin for viewing at the funeral, arrange for transportation, and cover the coffin with earth at the grave.

It is a long procession to the *Graabhof* (graveyard), and this time Nancy sits close to her grand-

father, clutching his sleeve with one hand. It is the first funeral she has attended, and she watches the grieving relatives, trying to understand, and feeling very helpless inside. She, too, realizes that Grandfather is old, and she, especially, is close to him.

Living in the *Grossdawdy* house alone since his wife died, but taking his meals with the others, Jonas has a definite place in the family. Since he became arthritic, however, he has confined himself to the lighter chores about the place, and has been a special companion to Danny and Nancy. Most older persons have a hobby, such as wood carving or rug making. Jonas is expert at making cane furniture, and Nancy has a little table and chair made especially for her.

The line of horses is long. With two hundred or

more buggies in the caravan, it takes a long time
for the procession to start. One horse is hitched to
the hearse which is slightly larger than a market
wagon, its sides solid rather than canvas. A relative
climbs to the seat and picks up the reins, and the
line begins to move. At six miles an hour, a carriage
length apart, it is sometime before the hearse reaches
the Amish cemetery.

At the grave, there is no tent over the hole in the
earth, nor are there flowers. Kinfolk twist the screw-
driver which fastens down the top half of the coffin,
let down the box, and fill the hole up with dirt.
Later a small unadorned stone slab will be placed
at the head of the grave by a relative, with the name
and the dates of birth and death. But now the people
leave, and head back to the funeral dinner.

Again, the tables will seat only a hundred at one time. The first hundred to arrive begin eating. They are served only cold meats, some cooked vegetables, pickles, and dessert. At a smaller funeral, there might be a hot dish as well, but that is too much to manage for a crowd like this. Sometimes as many as nine hundred people attend a funeral. The women move swiftly to serve the first diners, who leave the table as soon as they have eaten to make room for the next hundred. Plates are rinsed hastily, tumblers are simply refilled. No one minds, and the crowd is quiet. The dinner—the meeting again with caring friends and relatives—gives support and comfort to Martha's daughter and her family, and reminds them that they are secure in the friendship of their neighbors and the fellowship of the Amish faith.

There will be a simple obituary in the village newspaper, and a year later—in memory of her mother—Martha's daughter will send the following item to the *Sugarcreek Budget*:

> "Her memory is a keepsake,
>   With that we cannot part,
>   God has her in His keeping,
>   We have her in our hearts."

Few such memorial poems are original, but are used over and over again, reworded to suit the occasion or the individual, and seem to satisfactorily express the feelings of the family.

Jonas does not like the thought of dying, but growing old has its advantages, for the aged are treated with great respect. Wisdom is believed to accumulate with age, and obedience to parents is one of the most frequent themes in Amish preaching. A man is thought never too old nor too wise to obey his father, and always cares for his parents in their declining years.

Like his acceptance of death, Jonas Stoltzfus has always accepted the possibility that there will be suffering in his life, possibly as the result of religious persecution. The Anabaptists, who were the forefathers of the Amish, were severely persecuted for their faith, and Jonas knows well the stories of their sufferings. Most Amish families have a book called, *The Bloody Theater or Martyr's Mirror*—1,582 pages of accounts of Christians condemned to death for their faith. First published in 1660, it records burnings, stonings, crucifixions, live burials, suffocations, whippings, and the cutting off of tongues, hands, feet, and ears. Many are eyewitness descriptions with words of farewell to family and church. Jonas has read much of the book and so have his fathers before him. The songs from the *Ausbund*, which the Amish sing in Sunday services, also tell about the sufferings and faith of the imprisoned Anabaptists of the sixteenth century.

Jonas knows that the Amish faith itself was founded about three hundred years ago by a preacher called Jakob Ammann, who felt that the Anabaptists were falling away from the strict requirements of their faith. But beyond that, Jonas knows only bits and pieces of Amish history, for the Plain People are primarily farmers, not scholars. Reading the old German Bible daily, and listening to the preachers on Sunday, Jonas feels he knows all he needs to know, and asks no questions about why he should believe or live as he does.

Europe, in the sixteenth century, was going through a period of troubles. The Black Plague, serious economic difficulties, the constant threat of the Turks, and great social unrest made the common people eager for new religions and prophets to show them a better way of life. Peasants found themselves out of work because of the growing commerce with other parts of the world, and those people without homes or masters were ready to become followers of new leaders. To many, the problems seemed to be due to the authority of the medieval Roman Catholic Church and other traditional institutions. Intellectual unrest gave rise to new ideas.

In 1517, when Martin Luther posted his theses on the door of All Saints' Church in Wittenberg, he did not mean to start a new church but only to reform certain practices in the old one. Some people, however, didn't feel he went far enough, and wanted to reform even the reformers. Religious revolt broke into open flame throughout Germany, Switzerland, and the Low Countries. Reformation leaders, such as John Calvin, established strict rules of behavior for their followers.

Conrad Grebel, an outspoken young student of Calvin, became a leader of a very radical group called the Anabaptists (re-baptizers) because they opposed infant baptism. Baptism was only valid after the age of sixteen, they believed, when an individual could understand the commitment he was making to God. They wanted to go back to the early type of austere Christianity—little groups of Christians assembled in homes, living simply, obeying God's commandments, apart from all that was worldly. Disdaining cathedrals or church buildings, they also had no use for bells, organs, choirs, and fancy trappings. They renounced oaths, reveling and drunkenness, and personal adornment. The Anabaptists were also pacifists. They refused all military service and had as little as possible to do with the state. They were not merely a group of religious extremists, but represented as well the most radical social tendencies of their time. They refused to make any distinction of rank or class, declaring all men equal in the sight of God.

The Anabaptist activity was centered in Zurich, Switzerland. Their confession of faith, drafted on February 24, 1527 in Schleitheim, read, in part:

"A separation shall be made from the evil and from the wickedness which the devil planted in the world; in this manner, simply, that we shall not have fellowship with them and not run with them in the multitude of their abominations. . . .

"To us, then, the command of the Lord is clear when He calls upon us to separate from the evil, and thus He will be our God and we shall be His sons and daughters.

"He further admonishes us to withdraw from Babylon and the earthly Egypt that we may not be partakers of the pain and suffering which the Lord will bring upon them. . . ."

Meanwhile, in the Netherlands, a brilliant Catholic priest, Menno Simons, found it more and more difficult to defend the actions of the Roman Catholic Church. One day he witnessed the horrible massacre of 300 Protestant "heretics," including women and children, who were fleeing from their homes in Belgium. He began denouncing such persecution from the pulpit, and in 1535 he and many members of his congregation broke entirely with Rome. They became known as "Mennonites."

The military might of the combined church and state was used against the growing surge of dissenters, and the Anabaptists and Mennonites were seen as a real threat, despite their non-resistance. Living defenseless against this onslaught, Grebel's and Menno Simons's followers were harried, persecuted, and tortured. Many were killed. Some were burned at the stake or tied to wagon wheels. The Anabaptists were persecuted almost as bitterly by the Protestants as by the Catholics. Luther and other reformers feared that such radicals would weaken the whole movement for reform because their ideas were so extreme. Calvin's followers even took Anabaptists out into Lake Geneva and drowned them in a mockery of baptism when they refused to give up their new faith.

Among the first Anabaptists were some of the most educated and intelligent people of their time, many of them former priests. The continual persecution made them utterly dependent on each other, but it also caused them to distrust those outside their group, and they held their meetings under cover of darkness. Harried by civil and religious authorities alike, they finally began to flee. Mennonites from the Netherlands also migrated to other places.

Grebel himself died of illness when he was only twenty-six, but Menno Simons and his followers wandered from place to place. Simons drew up strict rules for his congregation. One was the practice of *meidung*, or the shunning (avoiding) of any member who seemed to be falling away from the faith, lest his weakness affect them all.

When peace finally came to Europe in 1648, the Mennonites were granted toleration. They settled down in Germany, the Netherlands, Switzerland, and Alsace, and became merchants and part of the well-to-do class. But the Swiss Anabaptists continued to suffer persecution for more than 150 years. With their original leadership gone, their creative and intellectual character vanished and they settled into the mountainous regions, away from cities, as farmers. The term "Anabaptists" disappeared, and the name "Mennonites" was applied generally to include descendants of both Swiss and Dutch Anabaptists.

As prosperity returned, the old rules were relaxed. The Mennonites took a more liberal stand on *meidung*, saying it should be a spiritual shunning only, and did not necessarily mean that one could not live or eat with a family member who had been excommunicated (cast out of the church), for Christ himself was known to eat with publicans and sinners.

It was in this setting that the Amish broke away

from the Mennonites in 1693—97. A reformer arose
named Jakob Ammann. He was disturbed by this
loose discipline and felt that the Mennonites were
departing from the fierce pure faith that had guided
their forefathers. He preached a return to the old
ways and particularly to the *meidung,* insisting that
the excommunicated should be considered the most
dangerous of all sinners, and that none of the brotherhood should have anything to do with such a
person.

Young and aggressive, Ammann began holding
communion services with his followers twice instead
of once a year, and began the practice of foot-wash-
ing as commanded in the Scriptures. In the thir-
teenth chapter of John, the Bible tells how Christ
washed the feet of his disciples as an example of
humility, saying, "If I then, your Lord and Master,
have washed your feet, ye also ought to wash one
another's feet." Ammann taught that it was wrong
to trim the beard, and insisted upon uniformity in
dress, hats, shoes, and stockings.

He began an unofficial investigation of the congregations in Switzerland and nearby Alsace, asking
the ministers how they felt about certain issues,
such as *meidung.* He demanded unconditional answers, and if they did not fully agree with him, he
denounced them and succeeded in dividing the
Mennonites into opposing sides. He called for a
meeting of the entire Swiss ministry, and pronounced as excommunicated all those who either
did not attend or who would not subscribe to his
own views. Though he had no authority delegated

to him to decide what was right, he went about visiting congregations and banning those who did not agree with him.

Hans Reist became the leader of the opposing group, which believed that although communion could be denied to the excommunicated, *meidung* need not divide families or separate husband and wife.

Of sixty-nine preachers who took sides, twenty-seven sided with Ammann. Efforts made to reconcile the two groups failed. Ammann and his followers broke away from the Mennonites and became known as the "Amish." They were also referred to as the hook-and-eyers and the Mennonites were known as the buttoners, but the difference in dress between the Amish and Mennonites in Europe was never as great as it is in America today.

Young men of both sects, however, refused military service, and because of this, new persecutions came upon both the Mennonites and the Amish. Leaders were hanged, their houses and barns burned, and they were driven into wandering exile.

In America, the founder of the proprietary colony of Pennsylvania and member of the Society of Friends, William Penn, heard of their plight. In the early 1700's he offered them land west of Philadelphia. Many eagerly accepted this refuge and sent glowing letters to those who stayed behind. Owners of ships, eager for passengers, made wild claims for the new land. One advertisement, posted in the streets of the Dutch towns, read: "Many men in Pennsylvania own 500 geese. Bison peer from the forest. Giant deer stalk the woodland lanes. Two hunters stagger beneath the weight of a wild turkey. Indian corn grows free for the taking. Rye heads of prodigious size vie with beets and cabbages of tremendous proportions, and fish struggle to impale themselves on the hook."

And so the area was settled in 1709 by a group of Mennonites, and named for Lancaster, England. Swiss, French, Scotch-Irish, Welsh, and English settlers followed. By 1817, after more persecution, famines, and the Napoleonic wars, most of the remaining Amish left Europe for other lands, and many followed their forefathers to Pennsylvania. At the same time, other religious groups—the Dunkards and Moravians—were coming to Pennsylvania from the German Rhineland, and together with the Amish and Mennonites, became the forebears of the Pennsylvania Dutch. They were called Dutch because the word *Deutsch,* meaning "German," was misinterpreted. Of all these settlers, most belonged to the Lutheran or Reformed Churches. The Amish and Mennonites were only one group. It is to these other settlers that we owe the invention of the Conestoga wagon, the Pennsylvania (also called "Lancaster" or "Kentucky") rifle, and hex signs—not the Amish and Mennonites.

There are no more Amish in Europe today retaining the name and principles of the original group, for their descendants have reunited with Mennonites. The Mennonites in this country now number more than those in Switzerland, and there are many different orders, from strict to liberal. The

Amish share with the Mennonites the principles of Anabaptism, and both endorse the Dortrecht Confession of Faith, drawn up by the Dutch Mennonites in 1632. This document states that membership in the faith is to be voluntary, that adult baptism is to be the symbol of membership, that the members must refuse to bear arms or participate in government, both local and national, that there will be communion and footwashing among members, and that leaders will be ordained from the local group. The differences of opinion between the Amish and the Mennonites and also between various orders of each arise from the interpretation and practical application of these beliefs.

Old Order Amish see themselves as the inheritors of this revolutionary Christian faith. They see themselves as God's own elect, the one small group that through all the tortures and trials of faith has, by remaining separate from the evil world, held true to the New Testament faith. They believe they have built and preserved a real Christian society in a world of sin.

Like Jonas Stoltzfus, however, most Amish are not well versed in their history or why they believe as they do. The contradictions between what is taboo and what is not does not bother them. Custom is part of their religion, and the fact that things have "always been done this way" seems to give it authority.

In the nearly 250 years since the Amish migrated to Pennsylvania and other parts of the U.S., they have changed some, but very little compared to the rest of society. Time almost stands still for them. *Eppes Neies* (something new) is unacceptable to Jonas unless it is proved to be indispensable, as perhaps a new antibiotic to fight a stubborn infection. Things which simply make life easier or more convenient are not indispensable as long as one has the use of his hands and feet.

Danny's grandfather lives as his father and grandfather and great grandfather lived before him, and he hopes that Danny and his descendants will go on living in the same house, tilling the same fields, and keeping the same faith that he has known all his life. At the age of sixty, most Amish have enough money for a satisfactory retirement, and home is always home. This is all he needs. There is no question as to what is right and acceptable in Jonas's mind. He feels no need to know more than he does, and it bothers him that not all of his grandchildren feel this way.

6

baptism, Shunning, and Delinquency

It is Saturday night in Lancaster County, and Gideon Stoltzfus is hitching up his courting buggy and heading for the crossroads at Intercourse.

Horses are the love of an Amishman's life, and the Amish teenager values his horse as an outsider values his car. A son is usually given his first horse and buggy around the age of sixteen. The horse is a high-spirited creature similar to a racehorse, and Amish fathers drive a hard bargain when haggling for livestock.

Young men sometimes stud the harness with extra silver buttons. But when they officially join the church, they must give up the buttons as well as all other adornment and frivolous behavior.

Benjamin and Rebecca have mixed feelings about Gideon's going out on Saturday nights. They are fairly sure that many things go on that they do not know about. Some of the things which happen would upset them very much, although they tend to look the other way when his behavior is not exactly up to church standards.

Youth is the accepted time for rebellion, and parents know that their teenagers will go through a period of curiosity about things outside the faith. Rebellion usually consists of either running wild, or of increased Bible study and intellectual questioning. In terms of people leaving the Old Order, the latter is the greater threat.

Though many of the things young Amish do are not approved by the church, they are tolerated because the youth are not yet baptized and have not officially subscribed to the faith. It is better, the elders feel, to live frivolously before one marries and joins the church than afterward, for then he would be excommunicated and shunned. Parents also know that the sooner a son marries and takes on the responsibility of a farm and family, his work will occupy his time. And because all Amish get-togethers are arranged with a view to the boys and girls getting acquainted and pairing off, parents tend to overlook the noise and rowdiness and occasional complaints of neighbors.

Saturday night courtships are encouraged. Though personal adornment and pride in one's appearance are taboo, a young Amish girl hoping to attract a boy may daringly use a limited amount of beauty aids from the five-and-ten. Some wear glasses (with non-prescription lenses) to enhance their appearance, and if they want to risk a lecture, the frames may be somewhat fancy. Many make heavy use of perfumed soaps, and the boys often use scented aftershave lotion.

Pairing off at the village crossroads is not customary

in other Amish settlements, but is the tradition in Lancaster County. A few of the boys have dates, having secretively met their girls somewhere along the way, but others bring their own undated sisters and exchange them for other boys' sisters. An Amish boy with two sisters is assured of popularity. Sometimes as many as 200 or 300 buggies gather at the crossroads, and citizens have complained because of the noise and the buggy racing on the streets and highways from nine at night till three the next morning.

Courtship or *rumspringa* (running around) begins about sixteen for the boy and at fourteen to sixteen for the girl. After three or more dates, a young man may ask his girlfriend if she wants to "go for steady or for so?" A boy is often teased when his friends find out whom he is visiting, and sometimes they follow him to the girl's home and remove a wheel from his buggy, unhitch his horse, or even enter the house and raid the kitchen.

The recreation permissible for an Amish youth is limited. Spending money for entertainment is taboo. The only activities approved by the faith are attending weekly auctions, hunting, fishing, hiking, softball (except on Sundays), and the traditional Amish "sing," plus work-centered get-togethers such as apple *schnitzins* (apple-peeling and cutting parties).

The Sunday evening sing is the most common of all youthful gatherings, and often attracts Amish from other districts looking for mates. It is usually held at the same house where the church services were held that morning. A sing is not regarded as a devotional meeting. The young people gather in the barn, boys on one side, girls on another. There may be several hundred in all. If there are young married couples present, they sit in one section, *Mädels* (unmarried girls) in another, and boys sit on bales and haymows. The singing is conducted entirely by the unmarried. Only "fast" tunes are sung—popular hymns such as "He Leadeth Me," "Sweet Hour of Prayer," and "What a Friend We Have in Jesus." All are sung in German. Girls as well as boys announce the hymns and lead the singing. Between selections there is time for conversation. After the sing, which dismisses formally about ten, an hour or more is spent visiting.

In some areas, the sings tend to be rowdy in character and go beyond what the church considers acceptable. The last one Gideon attended, in another district, had only about a dozen persons singing. The other two hundred stood around indoors jostling and smoking, or were scattered about on the grounds outside. There are no chaperones when the young meet, and when a barn dance is scheduled on a certain farm, it is not even unusual for the parents to go away for the weekend. Corn-husking bees, threshing bees, and hay making have largely disappeared, as horse-drawn equipment and bailers eliminated the need for much of the hard work, and in many areas barn dances have taken their place.

Members of the group pair off and a square dance begins, with the holding of hands and swinging of partners. Though the Old Order faith prohibits all musical instruments with the possible exception of the harmonica, it is not unusual to find guitars, fiddles, and possibly even a record player at a barn dance. The impromptu band plays such tunes as "Turkey in the Straw," "Six-Hand Reel," and "Old Joe Clark," and at the end of the evening a collection will be taken to pay them, amounting to only a few dollars. The Old Order Amish prohibit dancing but do not consider these folk games as dances in the strict sense of the word.

Most of the youth are between fourteen and twenty-two years of age. Once a girl reaches twenty-three, her chances for marriage are slim, and some Amish girls must be content to be the second wife of an elderly widower or to go through life as a maiden aunt, like Gideon's Aunt Esther.

As the evening goes on, coats are taken off, possibly vests, and collars are opened, but hats stay on. Many of the young smoke cigarettes. The barn is full of dust as a few boys scuffle in the haymow, for about half have been drinking, and some are drunk. Below, in the tobacco stripping room, a poker game is going on. Outside, couples move about in the darkness, or sit by themselves in a parked buggy. The dance is not usually over till four in the morning.

Outsiders are definitely not welcome at Sunday night sings or other get-togethers. "English" persons are suspected of being there to spy and report wild behavior, and on one occasion an outsider was surrounded by a group of boys and beaten up.

Many families and church leaders are opposed to barn games because they have led to excesses, and often attract non-members with musical instruments. Such dances are viewed by some as unnecessary, frivolous conduct. The practice flourishes neverthe-less among some of the most conservative groups.

The barn dances do not particularly alarm Benja-min and Rebecca Stoltzfus. They would not like it at all, however, if Gideon came home drunk. And they would be especially upset if he were to buy a car, as some boys do, keeping it secretly in town, un-known to the bishop, and drag racing it on the high-way at night.

Delinquent behavior is evidenced in a number of ways. Around Lancaster there are many groups of Amish youth with their own distinctive names. There are the Groffies, the Ammies, and the Trailers, and these are again subdivided. The Groffies, for in-stance, are composed of still other groups referred to as the "Hillbillies," the "Jamborees," and the "Good-ie-Goodies." Occasionally there are disturbances be-tween these groups. One gang might cut the harness of another gang to pieces, or unleash the horses of the other gang to let them run off.

Some of the wilder youth have driver's licenses and own cars. They often take their dates to the movies in town. Some drink excessively and visit the bars. Others try to see how wild they can make their clothes. Harness cutting may bring retaliation from an opposing gang, and then there may be a vicious rumble. Some Amish youth have been known to steal chickens or grain and sell them or trade them for a dance floor for one night. Some show their rebellion by holding secret rodeos on a Sunday when the rest of the congregation is at worship. Sometimes the boys see who can swear the best, and they seem to have a

preoccupation with jokes about sex and elimination.

The Plain People receive little or no guidance about human reproduction. Amish parents purposely ignore any mention of it, especially in front of children. Not until marriage does a youth have a fair knowledge of sex information, which he has acquired piece by piece. Smutty stories and crude jokes can be told without attracting the attention of their parents, and are common among the boys. Sexual relations before marriage are disapproved of and condemned by the church. Transgressors are expelled from the faith and shunned for several weeks until reinstatement, which requires a confession before the congregation. The moral stigma does not remain with the individual, as sex before marriage is regarded as no worse than many other faults.

Many youth justify their actions by saying that their parents had a "high old time" when they were young. If they are not yet church members, they cannot be excommunicated. But parents sometimes feel that the youth are getting out of hand, and have various ways of controlling them.

They have been known to report a wild barn dance to the police and have the place raided, or to chop up a son's car with an ax. In one instance, Amish fathers got together and bought out a saloon where their boys had been going to drink.

Amish fathers are strict about the behavior they allow and that which they don't, and punishment is apt to be severe. If an Amish youth runs away from home, it is considered disobedience to one's parents

—a grave offense. Nonetheless, two obvious changes seem to be taking place in Amish life—a toleration for drinking, and the owning of cars by a rather large number of boys. A few Amishmen are alcoholics and some belong to Alcoholics Anonymous.

Though many Amish youth put off joining the church as long as possible—which gives them the freedom to own cars without risking excommunication—most eventually join and are baptized. At this point, the formerly wild youth quits shaving, gets married, and leaves behind him all worldly enthusiasms. Many of the wild ones become some of the most conservative members once they settle down. For this reason, marriage is the most joyously celebrated occasion. So valued is the married person that even though each member has one vote in the decisions of the church, the influence of the unmarried members is limited.

Amish youth cannot become church members until age sixteen. Most join about eighteen, and some as late as twenty-two. Elders of the Amish sect encourage parents to insist that each teenager seek membership in the church during the late teen years. Benjamin and Rebecca have already talked to Gideon about joining, since he is almost eighteen, but he seems to be in no hurry.

Young people are given an opportunity to join the church once a year. A class of instruction is held in the spring for all those who wish to become members of the faith. Ministers very simply acquaint the applicants for baptism with the Bible stories that show the right relationship with God. After six or eight periods of instruction, from May to August, a day is set for the baptismal service. Consent of the members is obtained to receive the applicants into fellowship. The applicants are told it is better not to make a vow than to vow and later break it. They are given an opportunity to "turn back" if they so desire.

Before the baptism ceremony, the applicants appear before the ministers in an upstairs room, and the oldest youth says, "It is my desire to be at peace with God and the church." Each of the others in turn says, "That is my desire also."

At the service itself, there are several hours of sermons before the actual ceremony. The deacon leaves and returns with a small pail of water and a tin cup. The Amish vow, to which the applicants must respond, consists of four questions:

1. Are you able to confess with the Ethiopian eunuch, that you believe that Jesus Christ is God's son?

2. Do you confess that you are uniting with the true church of the Lord?

3. Do you renounce the devil and the world with its wicked ways, and also your own flesh and blood, and commit yourself to serve Jesus Christ alone who died for you on the cross?

4. Do you promise to keep the ordinances (*Ordnung*) of the Lord and the church, to faithfully observe and to help administer them, and never to depart from them so long as you shall live?

The deacon's wife removes the prayer caps from the heads of the girl applicants. The bishop lays his hand on each head and says, "Upon your faith, which you have confessed before God and these many witnesses, you are baptized in the name of the Father, the Son and the Holy Spirit. Amen."

The deacon pours water into the cupped hands of the bishop and the water drips from the heads and faces of the applicants. Then the bishop takes the hand of each kneeling applicant in turn whom he greets with, "In the name of the Lord and the church, we extend to you the hand of fellowship. Rise up." Girl members are given the Holy Kiss by the assisting wife, male members by the deacon and bishop. The congregation is admonished to be helpful to the new members, and the service, now four hours long, ends with everyone kneeling for prayer, followed by a short benediction and hymn.

The vows of the Amish are not significantly different from those of other Christian churches. What is different is the promise to abide by orally-transmitted rules not actually stated in the vow. The Amish do not seek new members nor try to persuade others to join their faith. Anyone is free to join the church if he is willing to subscribe to the rules, but outside members are rare and would be considered something of a curiosity.

There are many influences for social control among the Amish. There is one's own conscience and the inhibitions against certain kinds of behavior. If this is not enough to deter him, his actions will cause immediate gossip, and if even this is not enough to stop him, he will be scolded by one of the preachers and then admonished by two ordained men. He will be required to confess his sin to the congregation—standing, if the offense is minor, kneeling if it is major. If he does not confess, he is "set back" (barred) from communion. If he continues the offense, he is excommunicated and shunned, possibly for life, unless he returns to the bishop and repents.

Meidung, or the practice of shunning, has been one of the most decisive factors in the faith. In some cases it does not bring the offender to shame and remorse, but drives him right out of the community.

The Moses Hartz case was an example of shunning. Moses was a prosperous, well-liked Amish farmer and preacher, who refused to shun his son because he had joined the Mennonites. He was "silenced" as a preacher, and later joined a more liberal church. After much controversy, and to the sorrow of many, Moses and his wife were shunned till their deaths by their Old Order neighbors and friends.

There are a number of such splits in families. Like Moses Hartz, many Old Order Amish are shunned if they leave to join a more progressive group. If a man of a strict order marries a wife of an order which does not practice the literal interpretation of *meidung*, he cannot join her group or he would be shunned by his old one, and because she may not like the strict practice of *meidung*, she will not join his. In some groups, the marriage itself would not be tolerated.

Some escape shunning by a very roundabout method, wherein they move to another state and

join another strict group, approved by ("in fellowship" with) their old group, but one which does not shun those who join more liberal churches. From there they join a still more liberal order with the consent of the second group and in some cases even move back to the old community to be with friends and relatives now without the risk of being shunned.

When a member is guilty of violating a rule, he is refused communion until he repents and confesses publicly before the congregation. If he does not, he will be excommunicated by the unanimous vote of the members. The bishop announces that the guilty party is cast off from the fellowship of the church and committed to the devil and all his angels. His only hope is not to die before the congregation relents and he can be reinstated, by vote of the congregation, after confessing his sins.

A "mited" or excommunicated Amishman or woman receives the worst punishment the community can inflict upon the unfaithful. He cannot eat in the same room with others of the faith. They will not speak to him nor do business with him. Friends will neither buy from nor sell to him, nor accept any favors from him. His wife must refuse him sexual relations. Few have the courage to risk such loneliness. *Meidung* is death as far as the community is concerned, but worse than death to many Amish parents. If a child of theirs dies in the faith, they hope to live with him in heaven, but if he rejects the church, he is lost to all eternity. Doctrine comes before ties with relatives and friends, and when a person leaves the faith, it is often a very emotional parting, with weeping and much grieving.

The well-publicized *meidung* case of 1947 involved an Amish farmer, Andrew J. Yoder of Ohio, who brought court action against Old Order Amish Bishop John W. Helmuth and two preachers, asking $40,000 damages and a court injunction against a boycott or *meidung* which he alleged had been organized against him throughout the Amish church.

The Yoders had purchased a car because one of their seven children had had polio and it was necessary to take her to Wooster frequently for treatment. The weekly thirty-mile round trip had become a problem by horse and buggy. The Yoders decided to withdraw from the Helmuth congregation and to join another group that did not forbid autos. But the old district still invoked a boycott on him, even though he had not been expelled, but had withdrawn peacefully. His own brother had been warned that if he did not shun Yoder, he too would be "mited."

The case attracted a great deal of publicity and the courtroom was packed. Outsiders found it incredible that Bishop Helmuth and the other defendants themselves arrived for the trial in a rented car.

The bishop and his ministers were unfamiliar with courtroom procedure and seemed very out of place. They had no lawyers to represent them and carried no notes or documents. The weight of the burden upon them brought them close to tears. They spoke of their extreme sorrow at having to invoke *meidung* against Andrew Yoder, but felt that their duty was clear and that they had no choice. Their order had always been lenient toward hardship cases, they said, and would have found some way to provide transportation for Yoder's daughter had he stayed in the faith.

In the end, the jury voted in favor of Yoder. The ministers were ordered to lift the *meidung* on him, and to pay the young farmer $5,000 in damages. Months went by and the bishop made no move to obey the court order. The county sheriff was then ordered to auction off some of the possessions of the bishop and preachers to pay the debt, and some things were sold before an anonymous contribution paid the remainder of the fine. A year later Andrew Yoder's crippled daughter died, as did one of the preachers and his wife. The year after that the bishop himself died. The entire case was a tragic one and left many open wounds in the community.

When a person decides to leave the Amish faith completely and "go English," it is also referred to as "going gay," or "cutting his hair." This is a sad time in an Old Order sect. If he is a landowner, he is asked to give up his farm and sell all of his animals and equipment. A father will not provide a farm for a son who "goes English," and a daughter who "goes gay" relinquishes her rights to the *Haush-dier* (furnishings) for her new home, which the bride's father always provides.

Because of the serious consequences of leaving the faith, the majority of Amish youth stay. Many who try their luck on the outside find life too complicated and strange, and return. A person who has "gone gay" and wants to come back, goes to the bishop, confesses and repents at a preaching service, and is voted back into the fold. The stability of the group, of knowing that one is secure financially, that he is presumed to be living the one true faith, and that he can count on the help of his friends and relatives should disaster befall him, is usually enough to keep the Amish at home.

There are some who do leave—those for whom security is not enough. John Byler, Gideon's cousin, is one of them. When he was nineteen, urged by the deacons and his father to join the faith, John decided he just couldn't do it. Lured by the countries he had read about in his geography text, he wanted to travel and visit cultures he had only read about before. He joined the Navy, and occasionally Sarah and Gideon would receive a postcard from him from a faraway place, with a few lines of greetings. Gideon never talked about the cards he received. Sarah silently put hers on the mantel for the others to read if they wished, and after a time Rebecca threw them away. Once, when John was home on leave, he stopped by to see them and stood awkwardly in the kitchen talking of this and that. The family postponed supper until he had gone. At no other time would a visitor not be invited to join the meal.

The day he left the community, Sarah and her mother cried as though he were dead, and unless he decides to come back, as some boys do after being away, he will be lost to the community forever.

7

Woman's Place in Home and Church

It is spring, and the rich Pennsylvania soil is warm and moist, ready for planting. On a certain Thursday, Sarah and her young husband moved to their new farm in another district, for the Amish almost always choose Thursdays for moving days. Now Rebecca is doing her spring cleaning, as it is the Stoltzfuses' turn to hold the Sunday preaching service at their home. Amish women are fastidious about their houses, and a few, who not only sweep the cobwebs from the barn, but sweep the road as well, are referred to by the others as "crazy-clean."

Rebecca is certainly not crazy-clean, but a large home with so many people living in it takes a lot of care, and like most other Amish homes, hers is a model of cleanliness and order. The rooms are painted in gray, and bare of mirrors, photographs or pictures. There is no wallpaper, no lace curtains, no fancy furniture. Oilcloth covers the table and linoleum covers the floor. It is a simple home, but the fences and yards are straight, the paint is fresh, and the barn and other buildings are in good repair.

The row of blooming plants on the kitchen window sill attests to Rebecca's skill as a gardener, and the fruit jars turned upside down in a long row over the picket fence, for storage, prove that she expects a good crop of vegetables from her garden this year. There may be as many as a thousand quarts of produce in her cellar by winter. A typical Amish pantry or cold cellar holds crocks of pudding, luscious bolognas, dried beefs, huge piles of potatoes and turnips, onions, and sweet potatoes, as well as jars of fruits and vegetables. The surplus is used for church affairs and for families devastated by unexpected emergencies such as fires and floods.

Outdoor ovens are still in use in some areas for drying fruits and vegetables, and for baking large quantities of pies and breads. Field corn is dried and browned in the oven before being ground into cornmeal. Rebecca is known for her baking skills, and, like most Amish cooks, prefers winter wheat for making pies and pastries, and spring wheat for baking bread.

Rebecca married Benjamin when she was only sixteen, and was pregnant with her first child by the following spring. An Amish woman's youth often disappears quickly, for life on the farm is hard, and she will probably bear her husband many children. Nevertheless, tourists to Amish country frequently remark about the look of contentment and serenity among the Plain People.

In addition to her household chores—washing on Monday, ironing on Tuesday, baking on Friday, and cleaning on Saturday—Rebecca makes most of the family's clothes, except for the hats and suits of the men and older boys. She does all her work without the aid of a vacuum sweeper, a dishwasher, an electric washing machine, electric iron, or electric sewing machine.

Though houses are jointly owned between husband and wife, the men seldom help with household chores except for butchering and apple butter making, and as cooks and table waiters at weddings. Women, however, often help out with farming chores, especially during harvest.

The Amish household is strictly monogamous and patriarchal, though marriages are by choice, and not arranged by parents. Women are not forced to marry someone they do not care for. Personal relations between husband and wife are quiet and sober, with no obvious demonstrations of fondness. There are few words of endearment or gestures of affection, though courting couples sometimes use them. Marriage is a bond of respect rather than personal attraction. The husband and wife are not regarded so much as a couple in love with each other as they are members of a group who must keep the dignity of the Amish faith.

There are few bachelors or old maids. Those who lose a spouse through death often marry again, and widows and orphans are always provided for. Divorce and separation are practically unknown, and marriage partners are completely faithful. When speaking of his mate to others, Benjamin refers to her as "she" or "my wife," but rarely as "Rebecca." She, in turn, refers to him as "he."

Arguments are few between the Stoltzfus parents.

Benjamin makes the major decisions and Rebecca rarely questions them. She is free to decide matters concerning the home, and Benjamin accepts her decisions. When they are displeased with one another, they express it most often by tone of voice or gesture, or sometimes say flatly why they are angry. Benjamin usually shows his anger by complete silence at the supper table. Once, Danny remembers, his parents did not speak to each other more than necessary for several days, and he was uncomfortable. But then it passed and life went on as before. There is rarely harsh or loud talk.

Family life depends on teamwork. "As one makes one's bed, so one lies in it," is the folk wisdom which describes their feelings about marriage and how it takes the efforts of both husband and wife to make it a good one.

Though pride is a cardinal sin, and Rebecca does not try to compete with other Amish women in looks or accomplishments, she values her cooking ability and the meals she prepares for guests, and is particularly fond of having friends and relatives for dinner. She is known for the variety of foods she puts on her table, and frankly considers Amish cooking superior to that of the "English." In a Plain home, the Sunday guest is urged to follow host and hostess' example by slipping his shoes off, stretching out on a couch or chair, and taking an hour's nap.

Home is generally a place of security as well as serenity for family members. Mates are valued when they are realistic about what they expect from each other, and are patient and courageous in time of hard-

106

ship. Children are very much wanted and though birth control is generally considered contrary to God's will, some Amish couples do use contraceptives. Birth, marriage, and death are the life ceremonies, and with the sometime exception of the first child, most births take place at home, often with the aid of a doctor, in the supporting presence of the father. There are no godparents, but many relatives are always ready to take the child should something happen to his parents. Discipline is strict, but children are generally treated fairly. Though Amish love their children greatly, there is not too much time to play with them, and childhood is over quickly, with no photographs to help parents remember them as they once were.

As a married woman, Rebecca wears a black bonnet and a black or dark-colored dress that must come exactly eight inches above the floor, no more. Her apron is black, and the white mesh *Kapp* (cap) is put on as soon as she rises in the morning and worn until she goes to bed at night. There are no ready-made dresses for girls and women. White-headed straight pins hold the top part of her apron to the bottom, covering her voluminous skirt. When she goes to town or to church, she also wears a black bonnet, called a "candle snuffer" by some. A head covering, whatever the form, is now a church ordinance binding all female members of the entire Mennonite and Amish churches, regardless of locale or congregational affiiliation. With some modern Mennonites, the covering is only worn in church.

Rebecca's hair is parted in the middle, then

brushed back and rolled, never braided, in a knot at the back of her head. She uses no mirror. Because the women and girls pull their hair back so tightly, many show signs of balding, and Rebecca, at thirty-nine, already has thin patches above her forehead and over her temples. Small girls are allowed to braid their hair, but it must not hang down from their heads. Children may also wear clothes with buttons until they are older.

The cut, the length, the number of pleats in a woman's dress—even the number of straight pins used—are all prescribed for Rebecca. There are to be no prints, stripes, or plaids, and women may not show any individuality in their clothing. In winter, Rebecca wears a full shawl of heavy black wool, and because button shoes are no longer available, she now wears black oxfords with medium-sized heels.

Not only in terms of dress, but as a wife and woman, Rebecca knows what is expected of her in both home and church. Though women have a vote in congregational decisions, the Sunday services are definitely run by the men. Women are neither or-dained as ministers of the church nor do they speak up in the service. When applicants are baptized, boys are baptized before girls. At the communal meal following the Sunday meeting, if there is not room at the tables for all, the men are served first. Men leave both the service and table before the women. It is also usually the men who vote in local or state elections, if the Amish vote at all. Men are definitely the privileged sex in this society, but this is the way it has always been done as long as anyone can remem-

ber, and so no one questions why it should be so, or whether it ought to continue.

The day of the preaching has come, and Rebecca is ready. With the help of other women, all food was prepared the day before. Only unavoidable chores are done on Sundays. Even the threat of thunderstorms at harvest time still cannot make the Amish work on Sunday. Milk may be heated for infants and coffee made, but that is all. The rest of the meal is served cold.

As people gather for the service, they exchange a handshake. All who are physically able must attend. Rebecca directs the women and girls to the wash house where they leave their shawls and bonnets. In summertime, the young girls linger here to visit until it is time to go in. In winter, they gather in the kitchen. They enter single file, according to age.

Benjamin and his sons take the visitors' horses to the barn and give them hay. It is here that the men leave their heavy coats in winter, for there are no closets in the house. Ordained men enter first, followed by the oldest men, then the middle-aged. The unmarried boys enter last and, like the girls, according to age.

Inside the house, women and girls sit to the left, facing the men and boys on the right, except for small boys who sit with their mothers. If a baby cries, the mother takes him outside till he quiets down, then brings him back. Many Amish have been attending Sunday service since they were four weeks old.

The ordained men sit on chairs, the older men get

the benches by the wall, feeble ones are given rockers. Ministers' wives and older women also get chairs. Everyone else sits on hard backless benches, which are carted from house to house and stacked on the porch till time to set them up. Depending on the district, men and boys leave their hats on, take them off at the first hymn, or remove them before they enter the house. Hats are also removed for silent prayer, which begins and ends the communal meal following the service.

The service itself lasts three hours or more. A *Vorsinger* (one who leads the singing) sings the first syllable of the first hymn, and the congregation senses the succeeding notes and joins in, singing in unison. The last syllable of each line is cut short, and there is a brief pause until the *Vorsinger* begins the next line alone in a shaky falsetto, which sounds somewhat like wailing.

The Amish hymn book, the *Ausbund*, derived from the Gregorian chants of Southern Germany, was first published in 1564. The book is 812 pages long, and contains only 140 songs, but not a note of music or scale. The 140 poems or hymns have an average length of sixteen stanzas. They praise the early Christian faith and memorialize the personal suffering and tragedy of the Anabaptists. Written as poems or testimonials of Anabaptist prisoners confined in the castle at Passau, Bavaria, they express great sorrow and loneliness, and the conviction that God will lead them to everlasting life.

To an outsider, the hymns would seem most monotonous because they repeat the same musical arrangements. The melody of each hymn is indicated by reference to an old tune which the Amish congregations memorize. The tunes are so complicated that it often takes years to learn to sing them well. Because they are not written down, they have been passed on from mouth to ear for more than 250 years. Each syllable of every word stretches over a number of different notes so that it takes a very long time just to sing a sentence of text.

The congregation continues to sing hymns with long periods of silence between them. Any member, if he desires, may announce the number of a hymn and proceed to begin each line, thus setting the pitch. A younger man is often urged to take over the singing of a familiar hymn, and if he falters, the others join in and help out.

The preachers confer together upstairs while the congregation is singing. The hymn stops at the end of the verse when they come down.

There is an introductory sermon by one of the preachers who often uses a mixture of Pennsylvania German, German, and English. This is followed by prayer, all kneeling, and usually silent. When the Amish pray, they turn away from the preacher and face the back of the room to show that they pray to God and not to the preacher. When the preacher feels there has been enough time for prayer, he gets up from his knees and the others follow.

The scripture is read while the audience stands. The Amish use a Bible printed from old plates which they themselves own and lend to the local printer chosen to do the work.

The main sermon begins without notes or books. It is often delivered in a stylized pattern, with the voice rising to a high pitch, dropping at the end. The preacher concentrates on only a few appropriate well-used Biblical passages. He makes no new interpretations, and accepts unquestioningly the traditional doctrine. Amish preachers like to compare their order with the persecuted Jews of the Exodus. Much time is also given to urging the young to join the church and not put off baptism.

As the children get restless, fathers and mothers amuse them by folding handkerchieves into white mice with pointed ears, or babes in cradles. They whisper to their squirming children to stop "rootching," and are relieved when Rebecca gets up and moves to the kitchen. She returns with a platter of "preaching pies"—small half-moon pies filled with dried apples (that don't drip). These are passed silently around to the younger children, followed by a glass of water. Water is also provided for the preachers.

There are testimonials to the main sermon by other ministers who might be present or by other lay members. Then there are closing remarks by the minister who preached, and another prayer.

The benediction follows, with the people now standing. At the end, when the minister says the words, "Jesus Christum," all bow both knees in complete uniformity. Now there will be announcements, such as where the next meeting will be held, who is getting married, and whether members should remain after dismissal for a members' meeting. Any matter brought up before the congregation must first be discussed and approved by the ministers. Minor offenses, such as permitting a picture to be taken, are sometimes confessed at this meeting. Finally, there is a closing hymn and then dismissal.

Some of the men set up the tables for the meal which follows and others move outside to talk about the sermon. The women quickly set the tables and load them down with home-cooked food: pungent yellow cheese; rounds of spicy homemade sweet bologna; clove-scented red beets in vinegar, pickles, and plump rusk made the day before. There is a bowl of thickly creamed pudding for every four persons, and each helps himself with his own spoon. All enjoy the visiting and fellowship that goes along with the meal.

Preaching services are held every other Sunday, and alternate Sundays are spent quietly at home or visiting friends. Ordained men often visit the services of other Amish orders on these alternate Sundays, provided they are "in fellowship" with, or approved by, their own order.

No loud noise is permitted on the farm on Sunday, such as hammering or loud yelling. Children enjoy the long period of play on the off-Sunday, uninterrupted by none but the most necessary chores. Time is spent reading religious writings and learning the German language or reading the old German Bible. The Amish feel it is their duty to read the Bible in High German, but find it almost impossible to understand, and make no effort to really study it.

The Plain People are good conversationalists and

it is customary to visit relatives without invitation. Visiting is so important that it is the topic most often discussed in the *Sugarcreek Budget* newspaper. Because Amish youth can sleep late on the off-Sunday, Saturday evening courtship is traditionally restricted to every other Saturday on those weekends when the girl has an off-Sunday.

Communion is also a very special occasion for the Amish, an expression of unity and peace with the *Ordnung,* and is held twice a year. For a district not to have communion means that there has been serious difficulty in getting unanimous opinion on important issues, and without unity there can be no communion.

Two weeks before communion, a preparatory service is held. Every member must be present. Ministers present their views on the *Ordnung,* the unwritten rules, and mention certain practices which are forbidden or discouraged. Each member is asked whether he is in agreement and whether "anything stands in the way" of entering the communion service. Faults are confessed and adjustments made between members who have disagreements. No person is to join in with hate in his heart, for the Amish believe firmly in I Cor. 11 verses 28 and 29: "But let a man examine himself, and so let him eat of that bread, and drink of that cup. For he that eateth and drinketh unworthily, eateth and drinketh damnation to himself. . . ." Members who are known to be guilty of minor offenses but who do not confess cannot take part in communion.

For the communion service itself, the bread is

made by the hostess, the wine by the wife of the bishop. Foot washing follows a prayer, men in one room, women in another. The Holy Kiss follows, a symbol of love and fellowship, practiced more among the ordained than the laymen. Only members of the Amish order are permitted to this very special ceremony—a reaffirmation of harmony and peace within the brotherhood.

Amish groups do not, however, necessarily feel this same peace and harmony with other Amish groups. There are numerous disagreements and controversies among the many orders which keep them from being "in fellowship" with each other. The strict or lenient practice of shunning causes one of the most bitter disagreements. Others differ over whether the service should be held in a church or a home, whether the people should be allowed electricity and cars, and on down to such details as wedding rings, spectacles, neckties, rubber suspenders, leather belts, and haircuts.

Numerous groups have splintered off along the way. A division occurred in 1868 between those who wanted to have buildings in which to worship and those who maintained that only homes should be used. Those who began to worship in simply constructed churches were referred to as Church Amish. The more conservative Amish, who continued to worship in homes, were called House Amish.

An Amish church building is very spartan. There are electric lights and an electric clock, a pulpit, and a small communion table covered with oilcloth. The oldest members sit up front, on benches at right

117

angles to the other pews. There are cradles in a back room for babies.

Church Amish may have telephones and electricity in their homes, but no radio or television. The House Amish are more numerous, but the Church Amish tend to look down on them with pity and occasional derision at their rigid rules.

Another division occurred in the ranks of the Amish in 1927 when a bishop named Noah Beachy declared he could find nothing in the Bible that commanded Christians to plow with horsepower while other farmers cultivated far more land and raised much more food by using tractors. The Beachy Amish, as his several thousand followers are called, left the main group and soon adopted automobiles, though they painted the chrome bumpers black to avoid being fancy. Today the Beachy Amish still drive only black cars, dress in plain clothing, have their own schools, and are as reluctant as the Old Order Amish to see their children attend public high schools. Unlike the Old Order Amish, they support missionary programs and are more concerned about the welfare of people outside their community. Their views have made the Old Order Amish bishops all the more determined to defend the strict traditions.

The various religious orders in a single county may be many, from the most traditional Amish to the most liberal Mennonites. There may be "Old School" Amish, Renno Amish, Zook Church Amish, Locust Grove Mennonites, and Belleville Mennonites, among others. Both Amish and Mennonites practice adult rather than infant baptism, non-resistance, refusal to bear arms and swear oaths, and refraining from public office.

The Amish today differ from the Mennonites mainly in the extent to which external changes have affected the groups. The Amish are more literal in their observance of certain practices such as fasting and shunning, in offering mutual aid, and in keeping their young on the farm. The Mennonites have been readier to accept change. They are technologically modern and accept higher education.

In some Old Order sects, such controversies as the cut of the hair, the size of the hat brim, or the use of a glass window on the side of the buggy are considered matters of salvation itself, and association with people who do things differently is forbidden. Rebecca must be exact when she measures her dresses to be sure the hem is no higher than it should be. Benjamin, when buying a new hat, must be sure that the brim is three and one-half inches wide, no narrower. Because the rules of living and dressing and behaving are so exact and the consequences of disobeying them so severe, Rebecca must continually keep in mind what the others will think of her if she considers anything different, and she scrutinizes them in turn for signs that they are slipping away to newer things. There is no room for individual taste in the matter, and changes, if they occur at all, must come about slowly by group approval.

There are no written records in the Amish church at all, except for births which are recorded in family Bibles. A change in congregational rules then, when it does occur, can become rigid church law, and in another generation or two, will seem as though it has always been.

In addition to housework and cooking, concern for the sick is of major importance to Rebecca, and illness becomes major news in the *Sugarcreek Budget*. "Cheer-up showers" are frequently listed, in which friends are urged to send cards and money to certain persons in the hospital. The Amish are frequently victims of obesity, digestive disturbances, and heart trouble caused by rheumatic fever. Some are troubled with hereditary problems because of the frequency of intermarriage. Farm accidents, too, are common. The Amish are frequently kicked by horses, and children are often hurt in a variety of accidents.

The Plain People have no taboo against good medical care, and hold doctors in high esteem, though no Amishman himself studies medicine. They tend to change doctors frequently, however. Most accept immunization, though some are reluctant to do so. They practice very little preventive medicine. The Amish favor patent medicines and home remedies first and often wait too long to consult a doctor, especially for children's sickness. Rebecca has remedies, which she got from her mother, for rheumatism, arthritis, constipation, and itch, and makes great use of teas.

For croup, her prescription reads: "Boil vinegar, and if it is a severe case, hold the child over full steam till he can breathe easily." When Danny got an infection on his foot, she applied a poultice of milk and linseed oil.

A few of the older Amish perform a kind of sym-

pathy-healing called *Brauche,* but the formula is kept secret. It consists largely of the silent repeating of certain verses at appropriate times. Laying-on of hands is a form of cure also not uncommon. Too often the Amish are victims of "quack cures," and they watch their newspapers and farm almanacs for advertisements of patent medicines.

The Amish are by no means free of mental illness. Mentally retarded persons are cared for at home in some instances, but neurotics are often urged just to "work rather than sit around reading so much." Neurosis is evidenced by the failure to marry or to find satisfaction in work, by frequent visits to the doctor, preoccupation with religious questions, and rigidity in attitude. The suicide rate among the Amish is as high as the national rate, and suicide is most frequent among the young men of the settlement. Sometimes it occurs because of marital difficulties, from which there is no escape. Whenever it happens, it is regarded as a disgrace.

As the wife of Benjamin and the mother of six children, Rebecca does not worry about whether life is satisfying or fulfilling for her. Employment for Amish women outside the home is rare, but Rebecca gets pleasure out of maintaining a small roadside stand at which she sells produce from her garden. Some Amish homes sell other homemade goods to the public except on Sundays, but Rebecca limits her wares to fresh vegetables. She uses the "honor system" and puts a box with small change on the stand beside the cabbages and beans and a list of the prices. "English" customers help themselves and make their own change when Rebecca is called away to help out in the fields or is busy inside with household chores. The cash nearly always balances.

Rebecca loves to sing, and the children have inherited their fine voices and sense of pitch from her. The Amish take great pleasure in singing together at preaching services and weddings, and often sing for an invalid or to show appreciation to a visitor for something he's done.

Everyone seems to have a hobby, and Rebecca is particularly skilled at making handsomely decorated cookies for special occasions. She used to enjoy "Sister's Day"—a time when the women with preschool children take them to a neighbor's home, and the women sew and chat while the children play outside.

Now that Nancy, her youngest, is in school, Rebecca does not need time away from her children. But she still craves the company of women with whom to visit while she sews and mends. Friends and laughter and plenty of good food make the time go faster and the work seem easier, the Amish well know. Rebecca looks forward to getting together with others who share her past, her problems, and the hopes the Amish have for their children.

8

Work Days and Seasons

At twenty-two, Noah Stoltzfus is his father's delight. He even resembles Benjamin, with the same curly hair and beard, the broad back and shoulders, wide hands, and the same blue, deep-set eyes. Moreover, he puts in a full twelve-hour day beside his father, sometimes more.

Noah works full time on the Stoltzfus farm and now receives monthly wages. Gideon also works for his father during the busy months, but part of the year he hires himself out to other farmers or carpenters who need helpers. Amish fathers keep all the wages their sons earn, usually investing it for them in livestock or machinery, until the age of eighteen or twenty-one. Next year, when Gideon is eighteen, he will be allowed to keep half of what he earns. When he marries or joins the church, he will be allowed full salary, which is one way Amish fathers keep their sons in the faith.

Sarah also worked at an outside job for a while before she married—house cleaning in another Amish home. Such maids are given the same privileges as the rest of the family, for there is nothing demeaning about physical labor in Amish society. Outside employment is regarded as temporary, but even Benjamin looks for it now and then. In the off-season when farm work is slow, he watches the want ads for laborers, and occasionally supplements his income by helping a contractor dig a cellar or demolish an old house scheduled to be torn down.

Noah looks forward to having a farm of his own. Amish boys begin working full time at age sixteen, and may earn several hundred dollars in the first year as a laborer or farm hand. From there, they go on to become a one-third share tenant (dividing profits with the farm's owner), then a one-half share tenant, then a cash tenant, and finally a farm owner themselves.

Benjamin has too little money and too many sons to buy a farm for each of them, but he hopes to find one that Noah can rent first and purchase later when he has saved more money. Noah would like to start out as a half-share tenant. He has worked hard for his father, and already has a number of pieces of equipment, as well as his own livestock. Benjamin knows that his son is looking for a wife. It is difficult to begin a new farm as a bachelor, for farming requires teamwork, and without a woman to cook the meals and preserve the produce, it is better for a single man to live with another family.

Finding a suitable farm is even more of a problem than finding a wife, for land is scarce. Lancaster, Pennsylvania, is the oldest Amish settlement in the U.S. and also the most conservative. Some of the

Pennsylvania landholders occupy farms that were acquired directly from William Penn or his land agent.

The land around Lancaster, having a limestone base, is considered one of the best farming areas in the country. Without the help of modern mechanization, the Plain People consistently produce the highest percentage of top quality crops per acre of any farms in the country, giving the area the name, "The Garden Spot of the Nation." So thoroughly do the Amish know the earth that old Jonas, when he first bought the Stoltzfus farm, took off his shoes and walked barefoot to test the quality of the soil.

The Amish attribute their material success in farming to divine blessing. Their formula is simply rotation of crops with plenty of manure, lime, and fertilizer. Their objective is simple—to accumulate sufficient means to buy enough land to keep all their children on farms and, subsequently, in the faith.

The search for land forces many Amish to migrate to Canada. Others are taking over eroded, tired land in the South, hoping to make the soil fertile again in Kentucky and South Carolina. Some have moved to British Honduras and still others are considering Alaska. If an Amish father has a large farm, he may divide it among the sons, but most Amish farms are already smaller in acreage than those of many "English" farmers. Land is available, but not always where the Amish want it. They want land next to their settlement, and sometimes they must pay extremely high prices for it. Because of the land shortage, some young Amish couples have begun to restrict the number of their children.

When moving to a distant place, several families

usually go together and vote for four ordained men to lead them. Two things are necessary to form a new settlement: there must be general agreement on the rules, and the group must be large enough so that the young can find marriage partners within the settlement.

Benjamin values his farm highly, for the Amish have the best-kept farms in Pennsylvania. The barn itself is an imposing white, two-story structure that tourists often stop to photograph. It is referred to as a "bank barn" because of the earthen ramp that is built on the side of one wall which makes it easier for the farmer to wheel in the farm equipment through a second-story door. The ramp also helps to keep the barn warm in winter. The ground level has a cement floor where the animals are sheltered. There is also a workshop on this level and a room where harnesses are mended, as well as a tobacco stripping room.

The second floor, or hayloft, is portioned into sections for feed bins and bales of hay. The gabled ends of the second floor are used to cure tobacco, and as a storage space for farm equipment. Hex signs are found on the barns of the Pennsylvania Dutch, not the Amish. They are not used to keep witches away, as believed, but are simply for ornament.

Noah and his father treat their tools with respect. At the day's end, they carefully clean and polish each one before putting it away in a special place in the barn. Their tools are made with such care that often they last through several lifetimes. When a young man marries, among the gifts are always a few used farm tools which he feels honored to accept.

With some exceptions, all farm equipment must be horse drawn or powered. There can be no rubber tires on either buggies or farm equipment, and seats must not have springs, for these are unnecessary luxuries. Benjamin has a variety of wagons on his farm. There is the closed-in family wagon or carriage, and the open courting buggy used by Noah and Gideon. There is also an open market wagon and a sleigh. The same chassis can be used for a number of wagon bodies, some of which Benjamin made himself. Others come from the carriage maker's shop.

The Amish carriage shops are booked a year in advance, for there are not many carriage makers left and few young men are interested in learning the business. A buggy, however, if cared for, will last twenty or thirty years. There are numerous traffic hazards for the driver of a horse and buggy, and the buggies themselves prove a traffic hazard to automobiles which round a curve and are suddenly confronted with the slow-moving carriages.

Each vehicle has lamps run by dry-cell batteries, ordered by Pennsylvania law. Glass reflectors are mounted on the rear, and there are also rear-view mirrors. A hand-operated brake clamps an iron block to the buggy wheel when needed in emergencies. Paint for the buggy is either black or gray, depending on the particular Amish order.

Behind the seat is a heavy waterproof lid which covers blankets, groceries, and an extra harness. A loosely hung sheet of leather protects the passengers from flying mud and stones. The rear curtain can be rolled up to let air through. There is also a roll-up on each side of the front seat, usually kept up except in the coldest weather. Some Amish wagons have glass window screens for cold weather use, and some districts allow sliding, windowed doors.

Manufacturers who supply some of the carriage parts say that their dies are wearing out, and there is not enough business to make it worthwhile to replace them. A new supplier might be found, but prices would be higher. It is possible that within a few decades, the lack of coach makers and carriage parts will force the Amish to allow ownership of cars.

Blacksmiths are spotted throughout the community to keep the horses shod. This must be done every three or four months, depending on how much the horse is driven on the surfaced roads.

With one team of horses, the best a man can cultivate is eighty acres, and the maximum Amish farm is about 160 acres. Acreage is limited by the amount of land available, the price, the number of different crops, and how intensely they must be cultivated. There are some advantages to horses instead of machines. For instance, an Amishman can plow his fields much earlier in the year than the non-Amish farmers, whose heavy mechanical plows would bog down in the damp spring earth.

Most farms have a driving horse, a work horse, and a draft mule. Driving horses serve their owners ten to fifteen years if properly cared for. Sometimes disqualified race horses are used for pulling the buggies. Work horses have life spans of twenty to thirty years, and may weigh from 1,000 to 2,000 pounds. They are used for heavy farm work. The draft mule is a

cross between a donkey and horse, and gives a longer work day with less water and feed than a horse. It is not as readily available, however.

Many districts allow the use of an ancient gasoline engine for odd jobs around the farm. This one-cylinder, portable engine can be hitched up to a corn sheller, washing machine, butter churn, silage chopper, or any number of other machines. Possibly the Amish feel they can accept the gasoline engine because it is considered old-fashioned by everyone else. When something is no longer available, a substitute becomes permissible. Because manufacturers no longer produce horse-drawn equipment, Amish farmers in many settlements have come to accept the cultivator, reaper, cutter, threshing machine, manure spreader, and disk harrow.

Massive old steam engines are also acceptable in some areas as a source of power. They are not to be used for tilling the soil, but can provide belt power in threshing and in filling the silo. They are also used in steaming tobacco beds to kill weeds and to purify the ground before the tobacco seeds are planted.

New ways of doing things which bring a greater economic reward have a better chance of being accepted than changes which don't. Agricultural ideas and practices which are not too obvious are also more likely to be accepted than those which are very noticeable. Amish farmers readily adopt hybrid seed, for example, but not contour farming.

When an Amishman buys a modern farm from an "English" person, he removes all wiring and central heating, but often leaves the kitchen faucet. Many owners will not allow the utilities to be removed until after the mortgage has been paid, however, and in such instances the Amish family is permitted by the bishop to live in the house and to use the utilities until the last payment is made. Then the electric wiring must be removed. In some districts, however, bathtubs are slowly coming in, and many families have running water in both kitchen and bath, pumped into a reservoir in the attic by the power of the water wheel. Some Amish use bottled gas. Most lights are kerosene, referred to as coal oil, and the Amishman buys it by the five-gallon can and plugs up the spout with a small potato. Though the Amish are not allowed electricity or freezers, they are permitted to rent food storage lockers in town for the meat which they butcher.

Amishmen often sell their milk to commercial dairies, but leave no milk to be picked up by the driver on Sundays. Many families churn their weekend milk into butter. Pennsylvania state hygiene laws require dairies to use standard milking machines. These are usually run by electricity, but many Plain farmers use gasoline generators. Milk is stored in metal cans and kept cool by cold water from nearby springs.

Benjamin Stoltzfus's farm is a fairly large one, and except for a few slack months, he and Noah and Gideon work from sunup to sunset. They practice five-year rotation of crops, and grow such a variety of things that there is always something to be planted or cultivated or harvested.

The Amish set high standards of work for themselves. Noah and his father are up at four each morning. Milking cows may take from one to two hours, and the milk must be left at the end of the lane for the milk truck to pick up. Breakfast is at five-thirty during the busy season, the noon meal at eleven, supper at four, and bedtime at nine.

In the spring, around March, grass fields are rolled over and flattened to correct the heaving from winter's frost, clover or alfalfa is sown, liming and harrowing are done, and vegetables are planted in the garden. And of course there are the farm sales and auctions which no farmer misses if he can help it. Spring is a time for planting potatoes as early as possible, for seeding the oat crop, and preparing the ground for corn planting. As it gets warmer, the corn is sown in the fields and tobacco is sown, transplanted and cultivated. Fruit trees, if sprayed at all, are tended to now, but because spraying equipment is so costly, much of the Amishman's fruit is purchased.

In the early summer months, the alfalfa, clover, and timothy hay are ready for cutting. Hay is stored in the barn, barley and wheat are harvested, grain threshed, and corn and potatoes cultivated.

August is the slack month. The family goes visiting and some Amish schools begin early, so that the children can be excused a few weeks later on to help with the tobacco harvest.

In the early fall, the tobacco is cut and stored, potatoes dug, corn cut and shocked, corn stalks shredded, silos filled, and steers purchased. As the autumn turns to winter, tobacco stripping begins and steers are fattened up for butchering. When work slackens off, it is time for farm sales, more visiting, and the many Amish weddings that occur in November.

Scarcely is Christmas over when the farm begins to hum with activity in anticipation of spring. Manure is hauled to the fields and spread as fertilizer. Apple trees may be trimmed. Plowing may begin as early as February. Harnesses are mended and greased. Young chickens are bought from the hatchery and placed in brooders. And so it begins again, the endless cycle of seasons.

On the Stoltzfus farm, there are ten acres of tobacco. The Amish have made the culture of this crop an art. It is an all-year, all-ages business that requires more man hours of hard work than almost any other farm product.

From each previous crop, Benjamin lets a half dozen tobacco stalks go to seed. He fills jars with the seeds and sets them on the sills of sunny windows. Nancy is encouraged to shake the jars repeatedly to discourage mold until sprouts split the seed hulls, around the first week in April.

Beds are prepared for the seeds by steaming them to kill any weed seeds which might be there. Steam engines are used for this task, and Danny and Simon are always on hand with a hatful of fresh eggs from the henhouse to bury in the seed bed just before the steam pan is tucked in. Later they leap into the hot loam and retrieve their hard-boiled eggs.

Before the sprouting tobacco plants are transplanted from the seed bed to the field, the soil is plowed, harrowed, and disked so fine that clods not even the size of a nickel remain. The tobacco planter consists of a pair of wheels and a driver's seat, a huge water barrel, and two low-slung seats. Planting tobacco is the job that Danny likes most. While his father or Noah sits in the high seat and drives the horse, Danny and Simon sit in the low ones. The machine plows two open furrows, squirts water every two feet into them, and in these wet places the boys each plant a tobacco seedling, one in each furrow. A board on the rear closes the furrow around each plant. Danny enjoys riding so close to the ground, smelling the fragrance of the rich earth.

The plants must be sprayed to discourage tobacco worms (cutworms) six or more inches long, horned, fat and green. All ten acres of tobacco must be hoed by hand, and the remaining shoots from the main stem ripped off so the growth will go into leaf rather than blossom. The black stain of the ripped shoots— the mark of tobacco farmers—colors Noah's and Benjamin's hands and must gradually wear off.

When the tobacco is ready to harvest, the stems are ripped off four inches from the ground. The leaves are left for half an hour to one hour, wilting in the sun, but not too long as they would have a bitter taste from "burn."

The stems of the leaves are speared on a lath. When the laths are filled, they are laid gently on the ground to await the long, narrow wagon called the tobacco ladder. Laths of tobacco are suspended on the wooden frame of the cart so that the tips of the leaves swing free. The tobacco is hung in the barn, still on laths. Tobacco sheds or barns are built with

slats in the sides which can be opened to give the drying leaves air.

The tobacco bouquet is pleasant and powerful. After the leaves become dry, they later absorb moisture from the air and become pliable again. Then they are taken down and stored in the tobacco cellar beneath the barn.

Stripping—pulling the leaves from the stalk—goes on in the stripping room most of the winter. Small children play there while their parents work. The leaves must be pulled separately from the stalk and put in boxes according to size. When a section is filled, the leaves are removed and tied into a bundle. A man working from cow-milking time in the morning to nine at night can empty perhaps a hundred laths per day.

Selling the tobacco is a tense moment. The tobacco buyers arrive on a certain day at a certain time to sample the crop and make an offer. Each buyer makes Benjamin only one offer. He will say yes or no. If he sells too soon, it can cost him perhaps a thousand dollars in comparison to what he might have received later on. But if he says no, there could be a quick end to the buying, and he'll have the entire crop on his hands.

Noah understands the problems of the Amish farmer. He knows that he will work far harder than his "English" neighbors with their mechanized equipment, yet he will earn no more. He can accept no government aid, no farm subsidies, no cash for crops unplanted, no social security. Nor will he borrow from a bank if he can possibly help it.

When Noah starts out on a place of his own, he will farm in the Amish way, according to the accepted rules of his faith and the teachings of his parents, for he is prepared to live his life as he has promised the church he would do. He is an example of the well-adjusted Amishman. Noah loves his work and finds great satisfaction in a job well done. He does not question what his father and grandfather have told him is right or best or wise, does not doubt his faith, argue with the deacon, or bother thinking ideas which are different.

Benjamin and Rebecca hold him up as an example to Gideon and Simon and Danny, but it is Simon whom they worry about the most.

Conflicts, Education, and Change

There were words at the breakfast table this morning —polite words, but strong, with a touch of defiance.

School had been dismissed for two weeks so that the Amish children could help with the tobacco harvest. Today is the first day back, but Benjamin has asked Simon to stay home another few days.

Fourteen-year-old Simon, sitting rigidly on the right side of the table between Danny and Gideon, stares at his father unblinking:

"I helped for two whole weeks. I did everything you asked me to."

"And a good job," Benjamin agrees, "but a few days more won't hold you back any. You're already ahead in your books. Nothing the teacher's going to say today you don't know already."

Simon does not move. For two weeks he has been counting the days till he could go back. He was studying the early explorers, and it has captured his interest like nothing else he has ever read.

"I *want* to go," Simon says earnestly, his lips dry. "I like it there."

There is no sound at all in the big kitchen. Old Jonas, at the far end, looks silently down the long table at his grandson, then at Benjamin.

But Benjamin Stoltzfus continues cutting his breakfast ham, eyes on his plate. "I need you another few days," he says firmly. "You'll be staying home today."

Danny thinks the matter is settled. He thinks that when Simon leaves the table and goes up to the bedroom that he is changing back into his work pants and shoes. But when he goes upstairs for his books, he finds the room empty. And when he reaches the school, he sees Simon already there, deep in the book on explorers.

Danny sits down at his desk and stares at his brother, as though seeing the tall, lanky youth for the first time. What is it that makes Simon so different from the others? Why isn't he content to plow the fields like Noah and drive the carriage like Gideon and quit worrying his parents and the deacon? What is it he wants that makes him so restless? Danny doesn't understand it. And yet, there are times he feels a glimmer of it too—times when he looks at the boys in the village and wonders what it would be like to "go English."

The education of his children, and the limits to it, is another great problem which the Amishman faces. Every Amish parent wants his child educated to a certain degree. He wants him to be able to read and write, work with figures, and be able to speak English fluently so that he can do business, when necessary, with the outside world. Beyond that, however, he sees very little value, and considerable harm, in more schooling.

The Amish believe that an eighth grade education is sufficient for all their needs. Pride of knowledge is considered one of the greatest of all sins, and there is little point, they believe, in knowing too much. Book learning (also called chairmindedness) is held in suspicion. They look at highly educated people as those who invented the theory of evolution as well as bombs to destroy the world, and so what is the value of such learning? "The more learned, the more confused," is Benjamin's favorite saying, and Simon is sick of hearing it. If an Amish boy grows up to be one of the best farmers in the settlement and a girl marries and raises a healthy family, they have attained the highest goals their parents hold for them.

State education departments have persuaded many Amish to go to public schools, and very few one-room schools are still operated under public funding. Those which remain are staffed with a state-certified non-Amish teacher, although the students are Amish.

Since most states insist that children attend school until age sixteen, which would be around the second year of high school, many conflicts have arisen between the Amish and state or local school boards. Most Amish attend public schools, but some settlements are buying many of the old one-room schools that are closing down, and running them themselves. The teachers are highly esteemed, and given full disciplinary powers. But the teachers, in the past, were often maiden ladies of the Amish sect who had only an eighth grade education themselves and were not, therefore, certified by the state to teach school.

In Pennsylvania, children were allowed to leave school at age fifteen if they were needed on the farm. Many parents had their children repeat the eighth grade, waiting till their fifteenth birthday, rather than go on to a public high school. Parents were taken to court, jailed, and fined, but still the practice continued. Some parents started their children in school at age seven instead of six so that they would reach age fifteen before they had to start high school.

In 1955, Governor George Leader arranged a compromise plan—the Amish vocational school. The pupils would perform farm and household duties under parental guidance after they had left the eighth grade, keeping a daily journal of their activities, and meet for classes several hours a week. These are usually held on Saturday morning from nine till noon, to teach English and arithmetic.

By the time a Lancaster youth reaches seventeen or eighteen, therefore, he has the basics of animal husbandry, crop rotation, and farm finances, equivalent to a college agricultural student. The teenage girl, after finishing eighth grade, learns homemaking.

Other communities, however, have not been so flexible. In the mid 1960's, in a small Amish settlement in Buchanan County, Iowa, school authorities forced their way into an Amish private school to compel the children to board a bus to take them to the consolidated town school. An an official reportedly remarked, "We are going to assimilate these people whether they want to be assimilated or not."

News reporters found out in advance what was

going to happen and were there to record the event as frightened children ran for cover in nearby corn-fields and sobbing mothers and fathers were arrested for not obeying the Iowa school law.

The Amish were summoned before the justice of the peace and found guilty of violating the law by staffing their own schools with uncertified teachers. The parents replied that when they sought and found qualified teachers, the school authorities either refused to certify them or offered the teachers more pay in town.

The parents refused to pay the fines on religious grounds, for this would admit guilt. They were warned that their farms would be sold to pay the fines, which were beginning to reach into the thousands of dollars the longer the parents delayed.

Finally Governor Harold E. Hughes ordered a truce of three weeks to explore alternate solutions. A longer cooling-off period of two years was provided when a private foundation gave $15,000 to pay the salary of certified teachers in the two one-room schools for two years.

Governor Hughes said, "I am more willing to bend laws and logic than human beings. I will always believe that Iowa and America are big enough in space and spirit to provide a kindly place for all good people, regardless of race or creed."

In 1967 the Iowa legislature amended its school code to permit a religious group to apply for exemption from compliance with the educational standards law. Maryland amended its school law in the same year so that Amish were classified as a bona fide

145

church organization and therefore not required to obtain approval of the Superintendent of Schools to continue to operate schools in that state. In Indiana the State Superintendent of Public Instruction encouraged the Amish to organize their own schools and develop standards in keeping with their religious faith.

Amish people are seldom fully informed about school reorganization plans, and they rely on the integrity of local officials. When taken to court, they can only state their position as best they are able: they fear that their way of life is at stake, and that their children will be absorbed into mass society through the values provided in the public school system. Benjamin has always feared a strong, progressive public school, for he knows that its aim is to make the child self-sufficient and competent, and perhaps moral without being religious. If a child feels he needs no one else, he may feel he does not even need the Amish community. Parents are particularly anxious that their teenagers be isolated from the outer world, for this is the time that youth rebel and test their powers against the parents.

The Amish show their children how much the parents need them when they are teenagers. The young person who works on the farm can understand the contribution he is making to his family. If he is in school most of the day, however, he cannot learn to appreciate the Amish way of life, parents argue. Benjamin and Rebecca do not just fear losing their tradition or even that Simon may "go English," but they fear most of all that their child will be lost to God and therefore they cannot spend eternity with him in heaven.

The Amish argue too that the religious and social aspects of their life cannot be separated. To deny them the right to educate their children as they think best is to deprive them of their religious liberty.

State and local school boards sometimes feel different about the issue. A state may insist that all children born within its domain have the same right to education and the same career opportunities which education affords. To have genuine religious liberty, a state may argue, children born in Amish households must be given a free choice of religion, including the option of breaking with the ways of their parents. By foreclosing higher education, the Amish deprive their children of the freedom of choice enjoyed by other young people.

In May of 1972, however, the Supreme Court decided in favor of the Amish. At issue was whether the State of Wisconsin could require three Amish children, who had completed the eighth grade, to attend high school until they were sixteen.

The case began in 1968 when three Amish farmers, Jonas Yoder, Wallace Miller, and Adin Yutzy, refused to enroll their children in the local public high school. Convicted of keeping the children out of school and fined a token five dollars each, the fathers argued that since the youngsters had already learned to read and write, they would not need further education to prepare them for the simple Amish life. The state of Wisconsin contended that children must have some secondary schooling to survive in modern American society and, more important, that shutting off the children from formal education after the eighth grade would effectively deprive them of the opportunity to move into the outside world if they wanted to.

By the strict beliefs of their faith, the three fathers could not fight the conviction, for this would not be "turning the other cheek" as Christ commanded. A small group called the National Committee for Amish Religious Freedom—including a Roman Catholic, a Lutheran, and some sympathetic ex-Amish—took up the case for them. *Wisconsin versus Yoder* was the first Supreme Court case involving the Amish, and the court held that the Constitution's First Amendment guarantees of religious freedom took precedence over Wisconsin's school attendance law.

"However strong the state's interest in universal compulsory education," wrote Chief Justice Warren Burger, "it is by no means absolute. . . . The conclusion is inescapable that secondary schooling, by exposing the Amish children to worldly influence . . . contravenes the basic religious tenets and practice of the Amish faith."

Justice Burger emphasized the law-abiding nature and self-sufficiency of the Amish and, most of all, their nearly three centuries of consistent behavior. "It cannot be overemphasized," he said, "that we are not dealing with a way of life and mode of education by a group claiming to have recently discovered some 'progressive' or more enlightened process for rearing children for modern life."

The court's decision seemed to guarantee that the

50,000 Amish—who lived in about twenty states—could continue to educate their children through eighth grade only. Had the Amish refused all formal education for their children, the ruling might have been different.

One of the most important results of the controversies has been the strengthening of Amish educational efforts. Not only have Amish built and staffed their own elementary and vocational schools, but they have gradually organized on local, state, and national levels to cope with the task of educating their children.

Intelligence test scores frequently show that Amish children are generally below national norms and slightly above those of other rural children. They score well on non-verbal tests, however, and show ability also in manual skills. And because their society differs considerably from the rest of the country, some might question whether these intelligence test scores are valid.

Simon Stoltzfus, like many other Amish children who love school, has learned that he must either become indifferent to it or run the risk of conflict with his family and the church. Today, however, as he sits at his desk and stares out the window, he feels he can no longer go on pretending that it doesn't matter. For Simon, reading and finding out the answers to questions matter very much, and now he has said so out loud.

An Amish child's education is strict. He is expected to be a good student so that the state examiners who inspect Amish schools will find the students' reading and writing up to statewide standards. But the Amish consider study of value only if it has a practical use, and learning for pleasure and fulfillment is wrong. Critical thought for its own sake has no function. The Amish prefer tradition over scientific knowledge, and for this reason relatively little science is taught in their schools, and only such history and geography as the state requires. The absence of critical thought, of reasoning and comparing, is not only approved within Amish society, but is actually a goal, and the sect as a group seeks to block intellectual development. The Amish are at peace with what they know, and feel that the things they do not know are of little value.

Not all Amishmen, however, can honestly feel so indifferent toward school and learning, and Simon is one of them. Over the years his resentment against all the restrictions has grown and in the last year or two he has felt increasingly angry and confused. He is a good worker on the farm, but he does not get the satisfaction from it that Noah does, and is eager to be finished so that he can read and study. Some of the "English" shopkeepers in the village like Simon and are sympathetic with his hunger for learning new things. A few of them have given him books on occasion, which Simon hides in the hayloft, and more than once his father has found a paperback book which Simon purchased with his own money. Simon finds himself thinking about the city library, and the wonder of walking in the place, lined with books, staring at the shelves and being able to select anything he likes. When he is angry, he thinks of his family as backward and uneducated, and then feels guilty and uncomfortable for feeling that way.

For youth like Simon, adolescence is a miserable time, not the reckless, carefree years which it is for Gideon. Simon wishes that many things were different—that there were more things to read in the house besides the newspaper, the Bible, and a few other religious books. He would even be glad for magazines occasionally, but these are not allowed either.

Simon's reasons for dissatisfaction are only some which exist among a portion of the Amish. Some young people resent the seemingly endless birth of babies into the family which they also must care for. Some long for a vocation or a profession which happens not to be acceptable to the Amish faith, or one that requires college or other special training. Amish youth sometimes find new meaning in another religious group and are converted. Many want the automobiles and fancy clothes which the rest of society enjoys. Some are simply curious, and desire more stimulation from the outside world. Many are upset about the practice of *meidung,* or bothered by the contradictions they discover in the Amish life style.

Contradictions are more apparent to outsiders and to the Amish young than they are to the elders. It is not at all uncommon to find a father who rides to Sunday preaching in a horse-drawn carriage while his son drives a car to a much larger congregation, doing his parents' errands for them during the week and taking them places in his car. Nor it is uncommon to find a son living in a house with electricity

and his parents living in another wing of the same house using kerosene lamps.

Young people note that their parents consider it very worldly to go into a bar in town and drink, but of little consequence if they drink beer behind the barn. It is taboo to have a phone in one's home, but all right to go to the neighbor's and use theirs. The Amish consider electricity and modern appliances as worldly, yet many homes have propane gas ranges, kerosene-burning refrigerators, automatic water heaters with a gasoline engine to keep up the water pressure, and fully-equipped bathrooms.

The more contradictions there are within a small society, the more people there are who do not quite fit the traditional pattern. And when a society begins to tolerate very many differences, or to wink at certain practices considered taboo, it means that more changes are sure to come.

Differences are quickly detected by the Amish. A boy can be rejected for baptism simply because he has some chrome rings on his harness or a hat brim which is slightly too narrow. In other instances, however, the opposite type of behavior is looked upon with disapproval. An Amish youth who quits smoking, or stops telling the usual dirty jokes, or gives up the rowdy barn dances is immediately suspected of fellowship with the Mennonites.

Of all the ways youth can rebel, association with the Mennonites or some other religious order is one of the most feared. Distrust of other church fellowships is so great that even expelled members will often not join other churches, but remain away from all church contacts completely.

Few Amish leave to become atheists—non-believers in God—but many find comfort in the promise of salvation offered by other churches. Amish object to calling themselves Christians because it implies to others that they consider themselves saved, and this, they believe, is something no one knows for sure until he reaches heaven. He can only hope for salvation.

In some settlements, young people have formed Bible study groups which attempt to renew the goals of Amish society from within. These groups are usually composed of those young people who do not want to take part in rowdy Sunday evening sings, and do not go along with smoking, drinking, dancing, or—in some communities—bundling (bed courtship). They also oppose the hoedowns, which are mostly music and beer and little singing. These young people are often dubbed "goodie-goodies" or Christians. Some become mission-oriented and want to preach the gospel.

In Bible study meetings they pray aloud, read and discuss the Bible, visit and sing in old people's homes, and conduct social get-togethers for the group. Offerings are taken for support of missionary work. Some groups try to remain secret because of opposition from the elders. One mother told her teenage son whom she suspected of leaving for a secret Bible study group, "We know that it can't be the Lord's will for the young folks to come together and study the Bible like that."

Amish youth are sometimes attracted to groups such as the Mennonites by what they feel to be their thoughtful, spontaneous, unhypocritical approach to religion. Some feel the need to know that they are saved now and destined for eternal life. Many are impressed with the personal testimony of such people, and also by their taboos against smoking, drinking, and other behavior condoned by the Amish but considered sinful by Mennonites. The Amish are ordered by their bishops to stay away from community revival meetings. *Fremder Glawwe* (strange belief) is the term Amish use for religions that teach an assurance of salvation, and any Amish youth who begins to argue about doctrine is considered to be too good, and comes under the suspicion of having a strange belief.

Back on the Stoltzfus farm, a disturbed Benjamin is driving another wagonload of tobacco laths to the barn. He knows now that Simon has disobeyed and gone to school, and his heart is heavy as he thinks about the boy. Why are his sons so different? Why is Noah so happy and Simon so restless? What are the chances of Simon's leaving the faith altogether?

Defecting young Amish men tend to make abrupt changes, such as joining the army or becoming converted. Estimates of how many young people leave the faith and how many stay vary. Far more stay than leave. In a study of one Amish church in Pennsylvania, John A. Hostetler found that 70% of the young people joined the church of their parents, and 30% did not. The more conservative groups lose the fewest members.

Some Amish young people who socialize with the Mennonites return to their own ways after a time, and look back upon the Mennonites as proud people with big cars. Slipping away for a fling at the world and then returning is becoming more common among the youth. Many take an occasional break now and then, cast off their Amish clothes, and travel for a time. Then they return, perhaps to marry and settle down, confess to the bishop, and are readmitted. Some, with a father who is too severe or punitive, simply run away and stay.

The "English" are more inclined to side with the youth who is attempting to break away than to side with the parents. Many of the outsiders who have friendly contact with the Amish—teachers, principals, missionaries, or older brothers and sisters who have left the faith—help bridge the gap between the settlement and the world outside.

Sometimes the youth are exploited, but usually the outsider wants to help the Amish make the transition. Many businessmen deal secretly with the young Amish so their parents won't find out. When arrested or convicted, Amish boys' names are often withheld from the newspaper if they request it. Postmen sometimes deliver their mail personally when they are delivering insurance policies or driver's licenses. Some are favored by the police, and let off for speeding or allowed to pass their driving tests before they are quite ready. Service station owners often permit the boys to leave their cars parked at the station overnight so the parents won't discover that they own automobiles. Increasing numbers of Amish boys go to bars or saloons, and there are few outsiders who are willing to cooperate with the parents in keeping their children in line, making the parents' job all the more difficult.

In many respects, the greatest weaknesses in the

Amish culture are also its strength, and vice versa. The prospect of a new line of thought appears to church elders to be antisocial or even criminal. This inhibits those who are original and creative, but at the same time it keeps out ideas which might cause trouble. Because they have placed a premium on stability rather than change, the Amish have achieved a fixed, almost static social structure in which time, as nearly as they can make it so, stands still. Their strong religious convictions, their use of a distinctive dress and language, and the strong patriarchal authority of the group has helped preserve their culture.

No society, however, is entirely free of change. The difference comes in the rate at which societies change. For the Amish, trends are slow. There are no gaps or sudden leaps from one way of doing things to another. One church took fifty years between adopting a moderate policy of *meidung* to adopting the automobile.

Social change is not change in one direction only, and changes in Amish society do not necessarily go from the conservative to the liberal. As some of the more liberal Amish groups become more lenient, some of the more conservative ones make the rules even stricter. Sometimes, within the same group, concessions in one aspect of the *Ordnung* are balanced by overconformity in another. If automobiles came to be acceptable in one order, for example, the rules about clothing might become even more strict.

A number of different situations set the stage for change. Amish sometimes try new ways when they

travel or move to a new place or even go visiting. Their outlook broadens. An Amish youth raised in an order where three buttons only are allowed on shirts might go to work for the summer for an uncle in another district where four buttons are allowed. Previously regarding four buttons as sinful, he may change his mind as he gets to know and respect his uncle. Occupations sometimes require machines, equipment, telephones, cars, or uniforms which were not acceptable before, and so pave the way for change.

Before a change is voted on, it has usually been discussed informally a long time by the members, and other small changes have preceded it. Finally one of the members violates the rule—he buys a car, for instance—and then possibly more members do so, until it becomes necessary to debate it in church and decide whether or not to change the rules.

When changes are being considered in the *Ordnung*, they must first be discussed among the ordained men in the district and have their unanimous approval before they are presented to the congregation. Decision making in the Amish Church requires taking the *Rat* (counsel) of all the baptized members. The men and women are polled separately. The members remain seated and either affirm the decision of the ministers with a nod of the head, oppose it, or remain neutral. Sometimes there is serious difficulty in obtaining a unanimous vote.

Changes are more likely to occur when the rules are not uniformly enforced for all members, when the attitudes of the bishop and ordained men in a given district differ from those in other districts, when a great number of members are leaving the order, and when leaders and parents tend to be tolerant of forbidden youthful activities, afraid that if they are too strict, their children will "go English."

There are many ways of allowing exceptions. Old people are often permitted privileges others do not have, such as inside toilets and possibly electricity, and these exceptions often lead to universal acceptance. Already many changes have taken place within Amish society: ball bearings have been adopted on carriage wheels and dairy barns have been remodeled to conform to standards required for selling milk to commercial dairies. Young men have often changed from black to brown shoes. Hair is cut shorter than in the previous generation. Mothers have substituted nylon for cotton material for some women's garments. Tractors for field work have been allowed in many districts, and there is a trend from general to specialized farming. In many areas the young are becoming interested in education and in occupations other than farming, and also in missionary work. Some Amish districts have allowed electricity, ownership of cars and telephones, and kitchens have been modernized with appliances.

Old Order Amish are conservative, and New Order Amish are more progressive. In the Old Order, tradition determines how the people behave and think, rather than how the feel about it. Vows in the Old Order mean what they have always meant. The Old Order Amish have always said no to more freedom and opportunity. They take a negative, defensive attitude, and change comes only when compelled on them from the outside world, such as state and federal crop regulations, barn improvements, taxes, and school attendance. To depart from the prescribed style is to commit the sin of pride or individualism.

The Old Order Amish show little interest in improving the world or their environment. In the past, many believed that Jesus Christ was an Amishman who spoke German, and that the world was flat. So firm was the belief that one Amishman took a trip around the world to see for himself, and came back to report that it was not flat after all.

Among New Order Amish, there is more concern and feeling of responsibility for the world outside the community. With a change in world view comes greater personal freedom and opportunity for intellectual activity. A climate of critical thinking emerges. Tradition is viewed as a block to progress. The New Order Amish develop a capacity for self-evaluation and self-criticism.

The more liberal groups also have had their controversies, however, over such things as the brewing of beer, modern clothes, resistance to civilian authority, use of the *Ausbund* or a more modern hymnal, four-part singing, musical instruments, and the use of German or English in the Sunday service or school. In all groups, liberal and conservative, the taboos are directed mainly against things that might form entering wedges that would split the rural society. Corn planters, for instance, are acceptable because they don't disrupt the farm life or lure the young to the cities. New Order Amish sometimes allow photos to be made of themselves and their farms if they are sure the pictures will not be used to ridicule them or any other sect of the Plain People.

Sometimes a group loses not only one member but the relatives as well. It is not uncommon for one or two children to leave the Amish faith and then the parents to follow. There are always new problems which cannot be solved by traditional solutions, and these cause anxiety and stress. Some districts discontinue shunning after two years, or if the person joins another Amish Mennonite or Mennonite group. Others try to keep a middle-of-the-road position in order to appeal to the young.

Controls are not so effective when the community is large and people do not know each other well. Warmth gives way to indifference toward those one does not know. When a change is made from House Amish to Church Amish, the after-service meals are discontinued. There is less time spent in face to face contact with other members of the community and more time spent in family and solitary interests. This strengthens the individual, but weakens the group.

Some sociologists have predicted the absorption of the Amish into general society within a few decades. The density of the population brings the Amish into closer contact with outsiders, and it is not so easy to be isolated as it once was.

All sociologists, however, do not agree. The Amish have already existed in this country for 250 years, changing relatively little compared to the rest of society. In a study (1967) of one Amish community in

Ohio, Harold Cross found that the population had the potential for doubling every twenty-three years. Families tend to be large. One Amishman, John E. Miller, died at the age of ninety-five leaving a total of 410 descendants. Another, Moses Borkholder, was reported to have 565 living descendants.

It is youth like Simon Stoltzfus who, unlike Noah and Sarah, have not yet found places for themselves in the Amish community. They do not feel really comfortable at home nor do they feel comfortable in the world outside either. They feel a need for more self-expression and individuality than the community allows.

The Amish feel that individuality tends toward "highmindedness" and self-praise. "Self-praise stinks," is a common Amish saying. Art expression is slowly creeping in on designs on chair cushions, antiques, and "show" china, but there is little other chance for expression. Young boys with musical ability sometimes play the guitar for barn dances before they become church members, and may be the new *Vorsinger* later. Those who have literary ability use it to a certain extent in school assignments or may, when they are grown, write up the news of their community for the *Sugarcreek Budget*. Boys with a scientific bent are urged to put it to use on the farm in raising crops or cattle. But if this is not enough, if a young person—like Simon—yearns for something more, he has nowhere else to go, nothing more to challenge him in the Old Order Amish.

Whether or not the Amish survive as a separate culture in modern America depends a great deal, perhaps, on how well they can strike a balance between the traditions that are the strength of the group and the need for self-expression that allows for fulfillment of the individual.

The Amish are not the only renegades from modern society, of course. The "back-to-nature" movement of recent years has attracted young and old alike to communes in search of a simple life of physical labor and homespun pleasures, void of pretense and frills. Countless groups have sprung up centering about tranquility, the quiet life, and the growing of organic fruits and vegetables. The difference is that while the latter groups tend to come and go, to change with the time and the mood, the Amish culture is based on an unwavering religious faith, custom, and tradition that has enabled it to maintain its self-sufficiency for nearly three centuries.

It is the end of the school day and Nancy Stoltzfus has already left for home, eager to bake the cookies her mother has promised she could do. Danny and Simon linger behind, in no hurry to do the chores that await them. Simon, with two books tucked under his arm, knows he will have to answer to his father for going to school that morning against Benjamin's wishes. It is the first time he has deliberately disobeyed, and punishment is certain. Somehow Simon felt he had to do it, and he knows he may even do it again.

And Benjamin, sitting on his wagon out in the field, the sun bearing down on his black Amish hat, watches and waits. Somehow Simon's gait and the awkward dangle of his arms sends a touch of sympathy through this Amish father. Having been young once himself, he knows the struggle Simon is having against his many restrictions. And being the father of six children, he knows the value of his way of life, and the need for conforming to keep it alive. If he allows too much freedom, he may lose the faith he holds so dear. But if he allows too little, he may lose his son.

And still not sure of what to do or what to say, he sits there alone on the wagon and watches the boy come home.

Bibliography

Brecht, Edith. *The Little Fox*. Philadelphia: Lippincott, 1969.

Budget, The. Sugarcreek: Sugarcreek Budget Publishers, Inc.

Burns, Edward McNall. *Western Civilizations*. New York: W. W. Norton and Company, Inc., 1949.

Cross, Harold E. "Genetic Studies in an Amish Isolate." Unpublished Ph.D. dissertation, John Hopkins University, 1967.

Denlinger, Donald and Warner, James A. *The Gentle People*. New York: Grossman, 1969.

Everett, Glen. "America's Sixteenth Century Teen-Agers." *Youth*. United Church of Christ. August 20, 1961.

———. "Amish Education and Religious Freedom." *Christianity Today*. June 9, 1972.

———. "One Man's Family." *Population Bulletin*. December, 1961.

Holy Bible. King James Version.

Hostetler, John A. "The Amish Family in Mifflin County, Pennsylvania." Unpublished Master's thesis, Pennsylvania State University, 1951.

———. *Amish Life*. Scottdale: Herald Press, 1972.

———. *Amish Society*. Baltimore: The John Hopkins Press, 1971.

———. *Mennonite Life*. Scottdale: Herald Press, 1972.

Knoop, Fred. "The Amish Know How." *The Farm*. Summer, 1946.

Miller, Cynthia. "Exploring a Conflict of Interest." *The Washington Post*, November 12, 1972.

"Pennsylvania County Industry Report, Lancaster County." Bureau of Statistics, Pennsylvania Department of Commerce, 1972.

"Right to be Different, The." *Time*. May 29, 1972.

Schreiber, William I. *Our Amish Neighbors*. University of Chicago Press, 1963.

Sorensen, Virginia. *Plain Girl*. New York: Harcourt, Brace, and World, Inc., 1955.

Steinmetz, Rollin C. *The Amish Year*. New Brunswick: Rutgers University Press, 1956.

"Victory for the Amish." *Newsweek*. May 29, 1972.

Warner, James A. *The Quiet Land*. New York: Grossman, 1970.

Wenger, John C. *The Mennonites in Indiana and Michigan*. Scottdale: Herald Press, 1961.

Index

175

178

PHYLLIS REYNOLDS NAYLOR worked her way through college by writing and selling her stories and articles. Over 1,500 have been published in magazines, and AN AMISH FAMILY is her twentieth children's book.

Mrs. Naylor likes to travel with her husband and her two boys, especially when each plans a part of the trip.

GEORGE ARMSTRONG is an accomplished folksinger and piper, as well as a talented artist. He has done over twenty children's books—THERE, FAR BEYOND THE RIVER, was his first for O'Hara—and loves the challenge of researching his subject.

DUE DATE

APR 2 6 1991			
APR 2 1 1992			
OCT 2 6 1992			
DEC 1 9 1992			
APR 2 5 1997			
3-1-05			
			Printed in USA